E·A·S·Y
GERMAN
EXERCISES

Practice for Beginners

Ruth Rach

Series Editor, Brian Hill

PASSPORT BOOKS
NTC/Contemporary Publishing Group

Acknowledgments

The author and publishers wish to thank the following for permission to use material: Renate Alf for the cartoon, "Back in Town," *Brigitte,* June 1993, p. 118; Deutsche Bahn AG for the reproduction of train tickets; Mairs Geographischer Verlag for extracts from the *Marco Polo* guide, *Ostseeküste Schleswig Holstein;* Unicef, Deutschland, for use of an advertisement.

Every effort has been made to trace all the copyright holders, but if any have been inadvertently overlooked, the publishers will be pleased to make the necessary arrangement at the first opportunity.

Library of Congress Cataloging-in-Publication Data
is available from the United States Library of Congress.

First published 1994 by The Macmillan Press Ltd., Houndmills, Basingstoke, Hampshire, The United Kingdom

This edition first published 1996 by Passport Books
A division of NTC/Contemporary Publishing Group, Inc.
4255 West Touhy Avenue, Lincolnwood (Chicago), Illinois 60646-1975 U.S.A.
Copyright © 1994 by Ruth Rach and Brian Hill
International Standard Book Number: 0-8442-2531-2
89 ML 0 9 8 7 6 5 4 3 2

Contents

Introduction

Easy German Exercises is a new self-study resource for language learners. First and foremost it is designed to provide extra practice in reading and writing skills in a digestible, enjoyable, and easy-to-follow format.

The book is related to the content of the successful *Just Listen 'n Learn German* course and will certainly be welcomed by learners who are using or have used *Just Listen 'n Learn*, but it is of equal value to people who have had other exposure to the language. The book takes as its starting point the crucial topics you need when visiting or developing contacts abroad. So you find yourself involved in activities to help you when you are introducing yourself; describing your family, your job, or your town; asking for directions; shopping; ordering meals or making reservations; saying what you like or dislike; talking about your vacation; or saying good-bye.

The book is particularly appropriate for people who have made reasonable progress in listening and speaking, but who feel they now need something a bit more concrete to reinforce the vocabulary and structures they have learned. The activities, therefore, have been carefully selected to practice key language points in an enjoyable way.

Everything is carefully explained, and you should have no difficulty knowing what you are expected to do. At the end of each unit are full answers, so you can check how you are doing. These have been made as comprehensive as possible, so you can figure out where you went wrong.

Everybody works at a different pace, but on the average you should expect to spend from 1 to $1^{1/2}$ hours working through each unit. It is a good idea to have a dictionary handy to check on any words you don't know.

You might also find it fun to work on the book with somebody else in your family or with friends. Two or three heads are better than one, and you can help each other. You can work at home, on your lunch breaks, or even on the plane or train.

Easy German Exercises is ideal for practicing, reviewing, and developing your language skills in an easy way that nevertheless covers the ground thoroughly. When you feel that you have mastered the activities in the 15 units, you will have a sound base to make the most of your vacation, visits from friends, and the many situations where language skills open up formerly closed doors.

Brian Hill
Series Editor

1 TALKING ABOUT YOURSELF

Exercise 1

Vorname	*Micha*
Name	*Ernst*
Straße	*Wiener Straße 7*
PLZ Ort	*A – 2410 Salberg*
Land	*Österreich*

Useful word   **PLZ (Postleitzahl)**   zip code

a. What's the lady's last name?   ....

b. What's her first name?   ....

c. What country does she live in?   ....

d. Which town?   ....

e. ... and what's the name of the street?   ....

Exercise 2   Let's assume you're John Driscoll from 17 Dover Street, Wilmington, Delaware, U.S.A. How would you fill in the form below? You may come across such a form when registering in a hotel. Note that the street name comes before the number, and the zip code comes before the town.

Name	....
Vorname	....
Straße/Nr.	....
PLZ Wohnort	....
Land	....

Exercise 3 Each group of words contains one that doesn't belong. Find that word and cross it out.

a. Frau Fräulein Sohn

b. Mann Herr Frau Sohn

c. England Spanien Deutschland München

d. Morgen Abend Urlaub Tag Nacht

e. Urlaub Geschäftsreise Name

f. meine wohne komme arbeite

Exercise 4 *What's wrong here?*

Three of the sentences below do not make sense. Identify them and explain why (in English).

a. Ich bin Herr Müller, und dies ist mein Mann Klaus.

b. Ich komme aus Berlin, also aus Deutschland.

c. Dies ist mein Sohn Cornelia.

d. Fernando ist aus Portugal; Hussein ist aus der Türkei.

e. Herr Marks ist Engländerin.

....

....

....

....

Exercise 5   *True or false?*

Study the short handwritten text, and then decide whether the statements below are **richtig oder falsch** (true or false).

Ich heiße Sandra Blum, und ich wohne in Stuttgart. Ich bin im Moment auf Urlaub. Mein Mann Eduardo ist aus Spanien. Eduardo ist auf Geschäftsreise in England. Mein John Erasmus arbeitet in München an der Universität.

		R	F
a.	Frau Blum lives in Stuttgart.	R	F
b.	She's on a business trip at the moment.	R	F
c.	Her husband is called Erasmus.	R	F
d.	Her husband comes from Spain.	R	F
e.	Her son is called Eduardo.	R	F
f.	Eduardo is on a business trip in England.	R	F
g.	Her son works in Munich.	R	F
h.	Erasmus works at the university.	R	F

Exercise 6 *Which caption goes where?*

Supply each cartoon with the correct caption.

a. **Ich heiße Johanna, und dies ist mein Sohn Emanuel.**

b. **Ich bin Frau Stolz, und hier ist mein Mann Emil.**

c. **Mein Name ist Klaus Stein, und dies ist meine Frau Cleopatra.**

Exercise 7 *Questions and answers*

Match the question to the best answer by connecting the right pairs with arrows.

Woher kommen Sie?	Ich arbeite an der Universität.
Sind Sie Engländerin?	Ja, ich bin Frau Vollmert.
Sind Sie auf Urlaub?	Ich wohne in Konstanz.
Wie ist Ihr Name bitte?	Ich komme aus Berlin.
Wo wohnen Sie?	Nein, ich bin auf Geschäftsreise.
Wo arbeiten Sie?	Ja, ich bin Engländerin.
Und Sie sind Frau Vollmert?	Mein Name ist Riedel.

Exercise 8 *Crossword puzzle*

The answers for **a.** to **d.** have all appeared in this unit, and the keyword is something most people look forward to.

a. The time of day when most people get up

b. German capital

c. Most people have at least two

d. The opposite of **Mann**

e. Polite word in a request

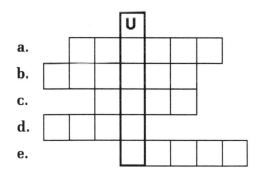

Keyword: ....

ANSWERS

Exercise 1
a. Ernst   **b.** Micha   **c.** Austria   **d.** Salberg   **e.** Wiener Straße

Exercise 2

Name	*Driscoll*
Vorname	*John*
Straße/Nr.	*17 Dover Street*
PLZ Wohnort	*Wilmington*
Land	*Delaware, U.S.A.*

Exercise 3
a. Sohn (the others are women)   **b.** Frau (the others are men)
c. München (the others are countries)   **d.** Urlaub (the others are
times of the day)   **e.** Name (the others relate to ways of spending
your time)   **f.** meine (the others are verbs)

Exercise 4
a. Mr. Müller can't introduce his husband, Klaus.   **c.** A son wouldn't
be called Cornelia, which is a typical girl's name in Germany.   **e.** Mr.
Marks can't very well be an Englishwoman.

Exercise 5
a. R   **b.** F   **c.** F   **d.** R   **e.** F   **f.** R   **g.** R   **h.** R

Exercise 6
a. C   **b.** A   **c.** B

Exercise 7
These are the correct pairs:

Woher kommen Sie?	Ich komme aus Berlin.
Sind Sie Engländerin?	Ja, ich bin Engländerin.
Sind Sie auf Urlaub?	Nein, ich bin auf Geschäftsreise.
Wie ist Ihr Name bitte?	Mein Name ist Riedel.
Wo wohnen Sie?	Ich wohne in Konstanz.
Wo arbeiten Sie?	Ich arbeite an der Universität.
Und Sie sind Frau Vollmert?	Ja, ich bin Frau Vollmert.

Exercise 8
a. Morgen   **b.** Berlin   **c.** Name   **d.** Frau   **e.** Bitte
Keyword: **Urlaub**

2 YOURSELF AND OTHERS

Exercise 1 *Telephone numbers*

Here is a transcript of phone numbers read out in various ways. Write them down as figures next to the words. You'll need to know one important word: **null**   zero (0).

a.   drei vier sieben fünf null zwo (zwei) ....

b.   sechs sechs neun eins acht sechs   ....

c.   neunzehn achtzehn elf   ....

d.   sechs dreizehn vier   ....

e.   vier null eins null neun   ....

f.   fünfzehn sechzehn sieben   ....

g.   vierzehn fünf zwölf   ....

Exercise 2 *Connections*

Connect the sentences with their correct translations.

Ich bin verheiratet.   I have a child.

Ich bin ledig.   I am single.

Ich habe ein Kind.   I am married.

Ich habe kein Kind.   I don't have a child.

Exercise 3 *A family*

Give them the right labels.

| Vater | Mutter | Sohn | Tochter | Kleinkind |

Exercise 4 Here is a short text about Frau Mohn. Read it and then check the correct multiple choice statements below.

> **Frau Mohn ist Lehrerin. Sie ist verheiratet. Sie hat einen kleinen Sohn und eine Tochter. Die Tochter ist achtzehn, der Sohn ist vier Jahre alt. Herr Mohn arbeitet am Verkehrsbüro in Hamburg.**

a. Frau Mohn is
- ☐ divorced
- ☐ married

b. She has
- ☐ a small son
- ☐ a big son

c. She also has
- ☐ two daughters
- ☐ one daughter

d. The son is
- ☐ four years old
- ☐ eighteen years old

e. Frau Mohn is
- ☐ a secretary
- ☐ a teacher

f. Herr Mohn works
- ☐ at the tourist office
- ☐ at the university

Exercise 5 *Male and female*

Fill in the blanks and choose the correct English translation from the box below.

♀	♂	
Studentin	....	....
....	**Verkäufer**	....
Direktorin	....	....
....	**Schüler**	....
....	**Rentner**	....
Arbeiterin	....	....

pupil	**retiree**	**salesperson**	**student**
worker	**director**		

Exercise 6 *Bin or habe?*

Complete the sentences.

a. Ja, ich .... Familie.

b. Ich .... seit fünf Jahren verheiratet.

c. Und ich .... eine Tochter.

d. Von Beruf .... ich Verkäufer.

e. Ich .... auch einen kleinen Sohn.

f. Ich .... seit zwölf Jahren in München.

Exercise 7   Here are the languages – but what are the countries?

a.   **Türkisch**   ....

b.   **Deutsch**   ....

c.   **Spanisch**   ....

d.   **Italienisch**   ....

e.   **Englisch**   ....

f.   **Portugiesisch**   ....

Exercise 8   Write the correct verb forms in the blanks. They are all scrambled in the box below.

a.   **Wie** .... **Sie?**

b.   **Ich** ....**Pia Fromm.**

c.   **Woher** .... **Sie?**

d.   **Ich** .... **aus Paris.**

e.   .... **Sie Familie?**

f.   **Ja, ich** .... **Familie.**

g.   **Und wo** .... **Sie?**

h.   **Ich** .... **in Köln.**

i.   .... **Sie andere Sprachen?**

j.   **Ja, ich** .... **etwas Spanisch.**

| wohnen   komme   habe   heißen   wohne   sprechen |
| kommen   heiße   haben   spreche |

Exercise 9   Here is a letter from Maria Ascher. Study it and then compare it to the translation below. Mark and correct the mistakes in the English text. There are seven mistakes altogether.

> Ich heiße Maria Ascher. Ich bin geschieden. Ich wohne seit zwei Jahren in Bonn und habe eine Tochter. Sie heißt Barbara und geht in den Kindergarten. In sechs Monaten kommt sie in die Schule. Ich bin Lehrerin im Kindergarten. Ich spreche etwas Englisch und Französisch. In zwei Wochen haben wir Urlaub.

My name is Maria Ascher. I am married. I have been living in Bonn for two months now and have one son and one daughter. My daughter's name is Barbara and she goes to kindergarten. In six weeks she will go to school. My husband is a kindergarten teacher. I speak some French and Spanish. In three weeks we'll take a vacation.

ANSWERS

Exercise 1
a. 347502 **b.** 669186 **c.** 191811 **d.** 6134 **e.** 40109 **f.** 15167
g. 14512

Exercise 2 These are the correct pairs:

Ich bin verheiratet.   I am married.
Ich bin ledig.   I am single.
Ich habe ein Kind.   I have a child.
Ich habe kein Kind.   I don't have a child.

Exercise 3

Exercise 4
a. married **b.** a small son **c.** one daughter **d.** four years old
e. a teacher **f.** at the tourist office

Exercise 5
Studentin	Student	student
Verkäuferin	Verkäufer	salesperson
Direktorin	Direktor	director
Schülerin	Schüler	pupil
Rentnerin	Rentner	retiree
Arbeiterin	Arbeiter	worker

Exercise 6
a. habe **b.** bin **c.** habe **d.** bin **e.** habe **f.** bin

Exercise 7
a. Türkei **b.** Deutschland **c.** Spanien **d.** Italien **e.** England
f. Portugal

Exercise 8
a. heißen **b.** heiße **c.** kommen **d.** komme **e.** Haben **f.** habe
g. wohnen **h.** wohne **i.** Sprechen **j.** spreche

Exercise 9
Here is the correct translation:
My name is Maria Ascher. I am **divorced**. I have been living in Bonn
for **two years** now and have **one daughter**. She is named Barbara and
goes to kindergarten. In six **months** she will go to school. **I am** a
kindergarten teacher. I speak some **English and French**. In **two**
weeks we'll take a vacation.

3 GETTING INFORMATION

Exercise 1   During the course of your vacation in Germany you have to write several checks. The words are written below. What would the figures be?

a.   Einhundertzweiundsiebzig Mark   ....

b.   Eintausendfünfhundertdreiundachtzig Mark   ....

c.   Sechsundneunzig Mark   ....

d.   Zwölfhundertachtzehn Mark   ....

e.   Hundertzweiundzwanzig Mark   ....

f.   Sechshundertfünfzig Mark   ....

g.   Siebenhundertvierundvierzig Mark   ....

Exercise 2   Now the problem is reversed. You have written out the figures but have yet to fill in the words – and you want to make a point of writing them out in German, too...

a.   DM 250,–   ....

b.   DM 317,–   ....

c.   DM 1 643,–   ....

d.   DM 297,–   ....

e.   DM 45,–   ....

f.   DM 72,–   ....

g.   DM 301,–   ....

h.   DM 613,–   ....

🅑 BERLINER BANK

Exercise 3

The dialogue below needs to be put in order to make sense. Write it out in the correct order in the space provided.

Eine Woche.

Ein Einzelzimmer.

Ich habe bei Ihnen ein Zimmer reserviert.

Mein Name ist Kröger.

Guten Abend.

Ein Doppel- oder ein Einzelzimmer?

Guten Abend.

Wie ist Ihr Name?

Ja, kleinen Moment bitte... Wie lange bleiben Sie bitte?

Sehr gut. Hier ist Ihr Schlüssel.

Bitte sehr.

Vielen Dank.

....

....

....

....

....

....

....

....

....

....

....

....

Exercise 4 You overheard the following conversation while waiting in the hotel lobby. Unfortunately you could not quite hear all the words. See if you can fill them in now. The words you need are in the box below.

Frau Kohl **Grüß Gott.**

Frau Lind **Grüß a. .... Was wünschen Sie?**

Frau Kohl **Haben Sie ein b. .... frei?**

Frau Lind **Ja, ein Einzelzimmer oder ein c. .... zimmer?**

Frau Kohl **Ein Doppelzimmer bitte.**

Frau Lind **Ist das mit d. .... ohne Bad?**

Frau Kohl **Mit Bad. Was e. .... das?**

Frau Lind **Das kostet siebzig f. .... pro Nacht.**

Frau Kohl **Danke g. ....**

Frau Lind **h. .... sehr.**

bitte	Mark	Zimmer	Doppel	Gott
schön	oder	kostet		

Exercise 5 Fill in the blanks below according to the example.

Example: *das* Hotel   ein Hotel

a. **das Frühstück**   .... **Frühstück**

b. .... **Etage**   **eine Etage**

c. **das Zimmer**   .... **Zimmer**

d. **die Bank**   .... **Bank**

e. .... **Schlüssel**   **ein Schlüssel**

f. **das Pfund**   .... **Pfund**

g. .... **Bad**   **ein Bad**

h. .... **Woche**   **eine Woche**

Exercise 6   In each group of four words there are two pairs. Can you match them?

Example: **Zimmer**   **Woche**
              Tag   **Bad**

a.   **Stock**   **Bank**
      Etage   **Verkehrsbüro**

b.   **Dusche**   **Bad**
      Abend   **Tag**

c.   **wechseln**   **Balkon**
      Telefon   **Pfund**

d.   **Rentner**   **Sekretärin**
      Postbeamter **Direktorin**

e.   **Schein**   **reservieren**
      Zimmer   **Kasse**

f.   **ist**   **hast**
      habe   **sind**

Exercise 7 Take a look at the price list and features of the **Hotel Gasthof Zur Grenze**. You won't need to understand all the words to be able to answer the questions below.

Useful words   **Haustiere** pets
Haarfön hair dryer

a. How much would you pay for a standard double room with bath, shower, toilet, and balcony?

....

b. Is breakfast included in the price?
☐ yes   ☐ no

c. What would you pay for a single room? ....

d. Do all the rooms have a clock radio, telephone and color TV?
☐ yes   ☐ no

e. Are children under six free of charge?
☐ yes   ☐ no

f. How many rooms does the family room have?
☐ two single bedrooms
☐ two double bedrooms

g. What would you pay for an additional breakfast?

....

h. Are pets free of charge?
☐ yes   ☐ no

Fam. Fiederer
Schanz 103 · 8999 Malerhöfen
Telefon (07562) 3645 · Telefax (07562) 55401

Zimmerpreise inkl. Frühstücksbuffet pro Tag:

Einzelzimmer - Bad/Dusche/WC	**DM 75,00**
Doppelzimmer Typ A - Bad/Dusche/WC	**DM 130,00**
Doppelzimmer Typ B - Bad/Dusche/WC/Balkon	**DM 140,00**
Doppelzimmer Typ C großes Zimmer mit Sitzgruppe, Bad/WC/Balkon	**DM 150,00**
Dreibettzimmer - Bad/WC, Sitzgruppe	**DM 180,00**
Familienzimmer zwei Doppelzimmer, verbunden durch eine kleine Diele, mit Bad/WC/Balkon	**DM 240,00**
Appartement - Bad/WC/Balkon, Doppelzimmer und großes Wohnzimmer	**DM 200,00**

Kinderermäßigung: bis 6 Jahre kostenlos im Elternschlafzimmer

Alle Zimmer sind mit Weckradio, Direktwahltelefon, Farb-TV, Haarfön, Kosmetikspiegel ausgestattet.

Sonstige Preise	**Pro Person/Tag**
Halbpension (3-Gang-Menü)	DM 28,00
Extrafrühstück	DM 14,50
Zusatzbett incl. Frühstück	DM 40,00
Haustiere	DM 13,00
Garage	DM 6,00
Kurtaxe	DM ,80
Telefoneinheit	DM ,60

ANSWERS

Exercise 1
a. DM 172,–   **b.** DM 1 583,–   **c.** DM 96,–   **d.** DM 1 218,–
e. DM 122,–   **f.** DM 650,–   **g.** DM 744,–

Exercise 2
a. Zweihundertfünfzig Mark   **b.** Dreihundertsiebzehn Mark
c. Eintausendsechshundertdreiundvierzig Mark
d. Zweihundertsiebenundneunzig Mark   **e.** Fünfundvierzig Mark
f. Zweiundsiebzig Mark   **g.** Dreihundertundeine Mark
h. Sechshundertdreizehn Mark

Exercise 3

Guten Abend.
Guten Abend.
Ich habe bei Ihnen ein Zimmer reserviert.
Wie ist Ihr Name?
Mein Name ist Kröger.
Ein Doppel- oder ein Einzelzimmer?
Ein Einzelzimmer.
Ja, kleinen Moment bitte... Wie lange bleiben Sie bitte?
Eine Woche.
Sehr gut. Hier ist Ihr Schlüssel.
Vielen Dank.
Bitte schön.

Exercise 4
a. Gott   **b.** Zimmer   **c.** Doppel   **d.** oder   **e.** kostet   **f.** Mark
g. schön   **h.** Bitte

Exercise 5
a. ein   **b.** die   **c.** ein   **d.** eine   **e.** der   **f.** ein   **g.** das   **h.** die

Exercise 6
a. Stock – Etage (both mean the same); Bank – Verkehrsbüro (useful
places for tourists)   **b.** Dusche – Bad (both can be found in
bathrooms); Abend – Tag (times of the day)   **c.** wechseln – Pfund (to
do with money); Balkon – Telefon (often found in hotel rooms)
d. Rentner – Postbeamter (men's job titles); Sekretärin –
Direktorin (women's job titles)   **e.** Schein – Kasse (to do with
money); Zimmer – reservieren (related to hotels)   **f.** ist – sind (forms
of **sein**); hast – habe (forms of **haben**)

Exercise 7
a. DM 140,–   **b.** yes   **c.** DM 75,–   **d.** yes   **e.** yes, provided they
share their parents' room   **f.** two double bedrooms   **g.** DM 14,50
h. no

4 ORDERING DRINKS AND SNACKS

Exercise 1   *Egyptian German*

Replace the symbols with the appropriate words from the box below.

Ich möchte gerne eine a. ☕ .... **Kaffee, ein**

weiches b. 🥚 ...., **ein c.** 🥛 ....

Orangensaft, und für meine Frau bitte ein d. 🫖 ....

Tee. Und dann möchte ich ein e. 🍰 .... **Kuchen,**

und für meine Frau ein f. 🌭 .... **brot.**

Kännchen	Wurst	Glas	Tasse	Stück	Ei

Exercise 2   Find the drinks hidden in the letter square below. You should come up with six beverages – across and down. We have already done one for you.

K	S	A	F	T	I
K	A	F	F	E	E
A	R	B	I	E	S
K	M	I	L	C	H
A	S	E	L	I	T
O	R	R	F	L	I

Exercise 3   Study the menu below – what would you order if...

Karte

Getränke

Apfelsaft ¼ l	2,50
Bier ½ l	2,70
Mineralwasser 1 l	3,50
Tasse Kaffee	1,60
Kännchen Tee	2,70
heiße Milch	1,70

Kleine Gerichte

Wurstbrot	5,10
Käsebrötchen	4,80
Rippchen mit Brot	9,70
Eiersalat	7,50

Nachtisch

Erdbeersahnetorte	3,50
Apfelkuchen	3,50
Käsekuchen	3,10

---

a.   You wanted a cold and refreshing alcoholic drink?

....

b.   You wanted a cold snack, preferably with some sausage?

....

c.   You felt like having a hot snack, but non-vegetarian?

....

d.   You'd like a hot beverage? It must be soothing rather than stimulating.

....

e.   You wanted a hot drink to wake you up in the morning? You don't like tea or milk.

....

f.   You'd like a dessert, preferably with fresh fruit, but no cream with it?

....

Exercise 4   Fill in the blanks below.

	Singular	*Plural*
a.	die Wurst	....
b.	....	die Brötchen
c.	die Mutter	....
d.	....	die Töchter
e.	der Sohn	....
f.	....	die Eier
g.	der Mann	....
h.	....	die Tage
i.	....	die Frauen
j.	das Auto	....
k.	....	die Biere

Exercise 5   Useful expressions in English and German. Pair them up as translations.

The check, please.	**Hier ist besetzt.**
Waiter!	**Leider...**
Keep the change.	**Getrennt...**
Enjoy your food.	**Zusammen...**
Unfortunately...	**Die Speisekarte bitte.**
This seat is taken.	**Guten Appetit.**
The menu please.	**Bezahlen bitte.**
Together...	**Herr Ober!**
Is this seat taken?	**Stimmt so.**
Separately...	**Ist hier noch frei?**

Exercise 6 *Detective work*

What's wrong with these dialogues? You can write your comments or suggestions for improvement in English in the spaces provided.

a. **Guten Tag, ist hier noch frei?**
Ja, hier ist leider frei.

....

....

b. **Sie wünschen?**
Ich möchte gerne eine Tasse Bier, für meine Frau ein Glas Kaffee und für meine Tochter ein Kännchen Saft.

....

....

c. **Was darf's sein?**
Ein Glas Apfelsaft und eine Erdbeertorte mit Salz, bitte.

....

....

d. **Haben Sie auch Kuchen?**
Ja, wir haben Wurstsalate, belegte Brote mit Salami und Wurst, und so weiter.

....

....

Exercise 7   Here are some words that can stand on their own, but they can also be combined to make new, compound words. Pair them up to create at least six new words.

APFEL   SAFT   KUCHEN

WURST   ROT

BROT   KARTE

ERDBEER   WEIN   KÄSE

SPEISE   BRÖTCHEN

....

....

....

Any more?

....

ANSWERS

Exercise 1

a. Tasse **b.** Ei **c.** Glas **d.** Kännchen **e.** Stück **f.** Wurst

Exercise 2

```
K  S  A  F  T  I
K  A  F  F  E  E
A  R  B  I  E  S
K  M  I  L  C  H
A  S  E  L  I  T
O  R  R  F  L  I
```

Exercise 3

a. Bier **b.** Wurstbrot **c.** Rippchen mit Brot **d.** heiße Milch
e. Tasse Kaffee **f.** Apfelkuchen

Exercise 4

a. die Würste **b.** das Brötchen **c.** die Mütter **d.** die Tochter
e. die Söhne **f.** das Ei **g.** die Männer **h.** der Tag **i.** die Frau
j. die Autos **k.** das Bier

Exercise 5 These are the correct translations:

The check please.	Bezahlen bitte.
Waiter!	Herr Ober!
Keep the change.	Stimmt so.
Enjoy your food.	Guten Appetit.
Unfortunately...	Leider...
This seat is taken.	Hier ist besetzt.
The menu please.	Die Speisekarte bitte.
Together...	Zusammen...
Is this seat taken?	Ist hier noch frei?
Separately...	Getrennt.

Exercise 6

a. It's very rude to say 'unfortunately this seat is not taken.' It's better just to say '**Ja, hier ist frei.**' **b.** You wouldn't order a cup of beer, a glass of coffee and a pot of juice. Normally, you'd order: **Ein Glas/ kleines/großes Bier, eine Tasse/ein Kännchen Kaffee und ein Glas Saft**. **c.** Strawberry cake with salt might taste rather strange...
d. The customer asks about cakes and is told about salads, bread and sausages.

Exercise 7

Here are some possibilities: Apfelkuchen, Wurstbrot, Speisekarte, Rotwein, Käsebrötchen, Erdbeerkuchen, Weinkarte, Apfelsaft, Wurstbrötchen, Apfelwein, Erdbeerwein.

Exercise 1 Match the German signs to their English equivalents.

a. | Ausfahrt | ....

b. | Kein Ausgang auf dieser Seite | ....

c. | Letzte Tankstelle vor der Autobahn | ....

d. | Umleitung | ....

e. | Alle Richtungen | ....

f. ....

A Last service station before expressway.
B Detour
C Exit
D Do not exit on this side
E All directions
F Bus stop

Exercise 2 *Sign language*

Interpret these station signs.

a. If you turn left, you'll find:

....

b. Straight behind you, you'll find:

....

c. Straight ahead of you, you'll find:

....

d. And to your right, you'll find:

....

Exercise 3   *Find the mistakes!*

Ursula Maier has written a letter to Frau Kraft on how to get to her house. There's a translation below, but it contains eight mistakes.

> Liebe Frau Kraft
>
> Ich wohne also jetzt in der Donaustraße Nummer zehn, das ist ein bißchen schwer zum Laufen. Es gibt auch keine direkte Busverbindung. Am besten nehmen Sie am Hauptbahnhof die Straßenbahn und fahren in Richtung Theater. Am Karlsplatz umsteigen, und zwar in die Linie sechs, das ist ein Bus, Richtung Waldingen. Und dann fahren Sie fünf Stationen bis zur Haltestelle Donaustraße und gehen geradeaus weiter. Ich wohne dann im siebten Haus rechts.
> Oder Sie nehmen einfach ein Taxi..
> Bis bald
>
> > Ihre Ursula Maier

Dear Mrs Kraft,

I now live at ten, Donaustraße, that's a bit difficult to drive to. There is no direct bus connection, either. The best thing is if you take the streetcar at the theater and travel in the direction of the railway station. Change at Karlsplatz to the number seven, that's a bus, direction Waldingen. And then you travel three stations to a stop called Donaustraße and turn right. I live in the fifth house on the left.
Or you simply take a taxi.
See you soon.
> Yours,
> Ursula Maier

Exercise 4   Here is some information on how to get to the **Kunsthalle**, an art gallery in Munich. Study it, then decide whether the statements below are **richtig oder falsch**. (H = Haltestelle)

WINTERLAND Von Munch bis Gulbransson KUNSTHALLE DER HYPO-KULTURSTIFTUNG MÜNCHEN Theatinerstraße 15, 80333 München Telefon-Programmansage (089) 22 78 17, Sekretariat (089) 22 44 12 19. November – 16. Januar täglich geöffnet von 10 bis 18 Uhr, donnerstags von 10 bis 21 Uhr	Folgende öffentliche Verkehrsmittel halten in unmittelbarer Nähe: Straßenbahn, Linie 19: H Theatinerstraße Omnibus, Linie 53: H Odeonsplatz U-Bahn, Linien 3, 4, 5 und 6: H Odeonsplatz S-Bahnen: H Marienplatz

a.   You can take streetcar line 19 and stop at Theatinerstraße.   R ☐ F ☐

b.   Or you could take subway line 3, 4, 5, or 6 and stop at Marienplatz.   R ☐ F ☐

c.   There is no suburban line to take you there.   R ☐ F ☐

d.   If you take the bus, line 53, you'll need to get out at Odeonsplatz.   R ☐ F ☐

Exercise 5   *Conversation with holes*

Fill in the missing words from the box below.

Sam   a. .... **Sie bitte, wo ist das Café Gindele?**

Ruth   **Das Café Gindele ist im Stadtzentrum, direkt** b. ....

der Kaufhalle.

Sam   **Ist das** c. .... **zum Laufen?**

Ruth   **Nein, zirka fünf** d. .... **Sie gehen einfach immer**

e. ...., **bis zum** f. .... **der**

Fußgängerzone, und dann sehen Sie die Kaufhalle auf der

rechten g. .... **Und daneben ist das Café Gindele.**

geradeaus	weit	Minuten	neben
entschuldigen	Seite	Ende	

Exercise 6 *Historischer Stadtrundgang in Ravensburg*

Historischer Stadtrundgang

1	Veitsburg	17	Weißenauer Hof
2	Burghaldentorkel	18	Hirschgraben
3	Mehlsack	19	Spitalturm
4	Ehem. Franziskane- rinnenkloster	20	Heilig-Geist-Spital
5	Obertor	21	Untertor
6	Haus der Großen Ravensburger Handelsgesellschaft	22	Altshauser Hof
		23	Pfarrhaus St. Jodok
		24	Pfarrkirche St. Jodok
7	Rondell am Gänsbühl	25	Vogthaus (Museum)
8	Hupishaus	26	Bruderhaus
9	Altes Theater (Brotlaube)	27	Gemalter Turm
		28	Stadtmauer und Wehrturm
10	Waaghaus und Blaserturm	29	Zehntscheuer
11	Rathaus	30	Untere Mang
12	Lederhaus	31	Grüner Turm
13	Seelhaus	32	Bauhütte
14	Kornhaus	33	Frauentor
15	Ehem. Karmeliter- kloster	34	Liebfrauenkirche
		35	Weingartner Hof
16	Ev. Stadtkirche	36	Konzerthaus
		37	Schellenberger Turm

You're standing at the end of the Herrenstraße marked X. Where would the various directions take you? Follow them on the map and fill in the destinations in the spaces provided.

a. **Gehen Sie immer geradeaus, und dann sehen Sie rechts die** .... **Das sind etwa 300 m.**

b. **Immer geradeaus, und dann kommen Sie direkt zur** ....

c. **Also Sie müssen geradeaus, die erste links, und dann wieder ein Stück geradeaus, und die zweite Straße rechts, das ist die Marktstraße, und dann finden Sie das** .... **zirka 200 m rechts.**

d. **Oh, das ist auf der anderen Seite der Stadt. Sie gehen die erste links, dann immer geradeaus bis zum Marienplatz. Am Marienplatz gehen Sie durch die Fußgängerzone, am Hotel Waldhorn vorbei, und dann die erste Straße links. Da sehen Sie rechts das** .... **und das** .... **Sie gehen geradeaus weiter, die Straße heißt Bachstraße, und dann sehen Sie rechter Hand das** ....

Exercise 7 *Odds and ends*

Match them up to form at least five new, longer words.

CAMPING   HALTE   HAUPT

ZONE   STRASSE   BUS

FUSSGÄNGER   STELLE   PLATZ

BAHNHOF   VERBINDUNG

....

....

....

Any others you can think of?

....

Exercise 8 Sometimes it's the little words that count. Complete the sentences below with the words in the box.

a. **Ich komme mit dir .... Bahnhof.**

b. **Sie wohnt .... Bahnhof.**

c. **Meine Frau ist bis 10 Uhr .... Theater.**

d. **Wir fahren .... Hauptstraße.**

e. **Reisen Sie .... München?**

f. **Gehen Sie .... die andere Seite.**

am	nach	zur	zum	im	auf

ANSWERS

Exercise 1
a. C **b.** D **c.** A **d.** B **e.** E **f.** F

Exercise 2
a. tickets, reservations, information **b.** suburban trains, subways, bus lines 40, 42, 43 **c.** taxis **d.** baggage check, luggage by rail, intercity courier service

Exercise 3
Here is the correct translation:
Dear Mrs. Kraft,

I now live at ten, Donaustraße, that's a bit difficult to **walk** to. There is no direct bus connection either. The best thing is if you take the streetcar at the **main railroad station** and travel in the direction of the **theater**. Change at Karlsplatz to the number **six**, that's a bus, direction Waldingen. And then you travel **five** stations to a stop called Donaustraße and **walk straight ahead**. I live in the **seventh** house on the **right**.
Or you simply take a taxi.
See you soon.
Yours,
Ursula Maier

Exercise 4
a. R **b.** F (you'd need to stop at Odeonsplatz) **c.** F (it stops at Marienplatz) **d.** R

Exercise 5
a. Entschuldigen **b.** neben **c.** weit **d.** Minuten **e.** geradeaus **f.** Ende **g.** Seite

Exercise 6
a. Liebfrauenkirche **b.** Kirchstraße **c.** Alte Theater **d.** Lederhaus, Seelhaus, Untertor

Exercise 7
Here are some possibilities: Hauptbahnhof, Campingplatz, Busverbindung, Hauptstraße, Fußgängerzone, Busbahnhof, Bushaltestelle, Haltestelle

Exercise 8
a. zum **b.** am **c.** im **d.** zur **e.** nach **f.** auf

Exercise 1 *Find the one that doesn't belong!*

Each group of words contains one that doesn't belong; find it and cross it out.

a. **Frühjahr** **Sommer** **Herbst** **Dienstag**

b. **morgens** **mittags** **zweimal** **abends**

c. **heiß** **lustig** **warm** **kalt**

d. **Dienstag** **Urlaub** **Freitag** **Donnerstag**

e. **Urlaub** **Woche** **Monat** **Jahr**

f. **Griechenland** **Spanien** **Italien** **Berlin**

Exercise 2 Translate as much as you can from the German signs in the store window.

....

....

....

....

Exercise 3 Decipher and rewrite the dialogue, putting in spaces, punctuation and capital letters as necessary.

a. GEHENSIEHEUTENICHTZURARBEIT?

....

b. NEINICHGEHEHEUTENICHTZURARBEIT. ICHHABEURLAUB.

....

c. OHUNDWASMACHENSIEJETZTIMURLAUB? FAHRENSIEWEG?

....

d. NEINICHFAHRENICHTWEG. ICHBLEIBEHIER.

....

e. SIEBLEIBENHIER? FAHRENSIENICHTNACHSPANIENODERITALIEN?

....

f. ICHMÖCHTENICHTNACHSPANIENODERITALIENFAHREN.
DAISTESMIRVIELZUHEISS.

....

g. UNDSCHWEDENODERFINNLAND?

....

h. DAISTESMIRVIELZUKALT. ICHFAHRENICHTWEG. ICHBLEIBEHIER.

....

Exercise 4 *Missing letters*

Complete the words below and the letters 1 to 7 will give you the keyword.

a.	F	¹ Ü	H	J	A	H	R
b.	²	R	L	A	U	B	
c.	³	E	R	B	S	T	
d.	S	O	M	M	⁴	R	
e.	M	O	N	⁵	A	G	
f.	M	O	N	⁶	T		
g.	T	A	⁷				

Keyword: ....

Exercise 5 *The clock*

Match the times with the pictures.

a. zwanzig vor zwölf (morgens) ....

b. elf Uhr zehn (morgens) ....

c. Viertel nach sieben (morgens) ....

d. halb acht (abends) ....

e. siebzehn Uhr acht ....

f. sechzehn Uhr neunundvierzig ....

g. neunzehn Uhr fünfundzwanzig ....

h. Viertel vor zehn (abends) ....

i. dreizehn Uhr fünf ....

j. halb sechs (morgens) ....

k. zwanzig Uhr dreißig ....

l. halb neun (abends) ....

m. Viertel nach drei (nachmittags) ....

n. acht Minuten nach fünf (nachmittags) ....

A **16.49**   H **11.10**

B **17.08**   I **15.15**

C **05.30**   J **20.30**

D **19.30**   K **11.40**

E **19.25**   L **17.08**

F **13.05**   M **20.30**

G **07.15**   N **21.45**

Exercise 6 *My vacation plans* – **meine Urlaubspläne**

Here is an extract from a letter by Agnes. Study it so that you get the idea of it, then answer the questions below in English.

> Dieses Jahr mache ich dreimal Urlaub, und zwar im Winter, Sommer und Herbst. Im Winter möchte ich gerne zwei Wochen nach Österreich fahren. Im Sommer, das weiß ich noch nicht genau, wahrscheinlich fahre ich drei Wochen nach Südfrankreich. Und im Herbst fahre ich dann noch eine Woche nach Barcelona.

a. How often does Agnes go on vacation?

....

b. What times of the year does she go on vacation?

....

c. When does she go to Austria?

....

d. What is she doing in the summer?

....

e. Is there a vacation in the spring?

....

f. When does she go to Barcelona? For how long?

....

g. Which is her longest vacation?

....

Exercise 7 Study the details of the restaurant Möhrenpick and decide whether the statements below are **richtig oder falsch**.

MÖHRENPICK	ÖFFNUNGSZEITEN	Montag Ruhetag
Vegetarische Speisen in rauchfreiem Raum	täglich ab 18.30 Uhr plus ... Mittagstisch Dienstag bis Freitag	Herrgottsgasse 10 88339 Bad Waldsee Telefon 07524 6647

a. The Möhrenpick is open every day.   R   F

b. The Möhrenpick is closed on Mondays.   R   F

c. You can get breakfast every morning.   R   F

d. It offers vegetarian food.   R   F

e. On the weekends it opens in the evenings only.   R   F

f. There are special lunchtime opening hours from Tuesday to Friday.   R   F

g. You can get Sunday lunch, too.   R   F

h. The Möhrenpick is a non-smoking area.   R   F

Exercise 8 Here's a dialogue about the opening times of the Municipal Museum. Study the information given, then complete the sign below by filling in the opening hours.

Hanna **Wann ist das Städtische Museum geöffnet?**

Annie **Das Stadtmuseum ist geöffnet – Dienstag bis Freitag von zehn bis zwölf und von vierzehn Uhr dreißig bis siebzehn Uhr. Am Wochenende, also Samstag und Sonntag, sind die Öffnungszeiten von elf bis dreizehn Uhr, und am Montag haben wir immer Ruhetag.**

Städtisches Museum	*Öffnungszeiten:*
.... *bis* .... : .... *und*	
.... *und* .... :	
.... :	

ANSWERS

Exercise 1
a. Dienstag **b.** zweimal **c.** lustig **d.** Urlaub **e.** Urlaub **f.** Berlin

Exercise 2
Top: Flowers all over the world – Fleurop
Left: Opening hours: daily, also on Sundays and public holidays
        from 7 A.M. to 9 P.M.
Right: Opening for florist
        Owner: welcome-flowers GmbH

Exercise 3
Here are the untangled sentences:
a. Gehen Sie heute nicht zur Arbeit?
b. Nein, ich gehe heute nicht zur Arbeit. Ich habe Urlaub.
c. Oh, und was machen Sie jetzt im Urlaub? Fahren Sie weg?
d. Nein, ich fahre nicht weg. Ich bleibe hier.
e. Sie bleiben hier? Fahren Sie nicht nach Spanien oder Italien?
f. Ich möchte nicht nach Spanien oder Italien fahren. Da ist es mir viel zu heiß.
g. Und Schweden oder Finnland?
h. Da ist es mir viel zu kalt. Ich fahre nicht weg. Ich bleibe hier.

Exercise 4
a. Frühjahr **b.** Urlaub **c.** Herbst **d.** Sommer **e.** Montag
f. Monat **g.** Tag   Keyword: **Ruhetag**

Exercise 5
a. K **b.** H **c.** G **d.** D **e.** B/L **f.** A **g.** E **h.** N **i.** F **j.** C **k.** J/M
l. M/J **m.** I **n.** L/B

Exercise 6
a. three times **b.** winter, summer, fall **c.** in winter **d.** she's
not sure yet, maybe she'll go to the south of France for three weeks
e. no **f.** in the fall, for one week **g.** in the summer

Exercise 7
a. F **b.** R **c.** F **d.** R **e.** R **f.** R **g.** F **h.** R

Exercise 8
Dienstag bis Freitag: 10.00–12.00 und 14.30–17.00
Samstag und Sonntag: 11.00–13.00
Montag: Ruhetag (geschlossen)

7 SHOPPING (part 1)

Exercise 1 Study the ad in the paper and decide whether the statements below are **richtig oder falsch**. Note that **Netz** means 'net' and **Steige** is a box, but these aren't words you'll come across often.

a. A kilo of bananas is more expensive than a kilo of oranges. R F

b. The potatoes are from Italy. R F

c. The grapes are black. R F

d. A kilo of clementines is cheaper than a kilo of grapes. R F

e. The potatoes cost DM 2,93 for 5 kilos. R F

Exercise 2 *Nonsense shopping*

Cross out the words or phrases that don't belong.

Ich kaufe mir heute...

a. **einen Ring in Gold oder Brot**

b. **zwei Pfund Weingläser**

c. **zehn große und zwei kleine Postkarten aus Silber**

d. **ein großes Kilo Brot**

e. **acht Flaschen Äpfel**

f. **und neun Liter Zwiebeln**

Exercise 3   Fill in the correct words from the box below.

Ich möchte gerne...

a.   **ein** .... **Pfirsiche**

b.   **ein** .... **Brot**

c.   **ein** .... **Kilo Kartoffeln**

d.   **ein** .... **Wein**

e.   **eine**............................... **Kaffee**

f.   **die** .... **Zwiebeln**

halbes	Glas	weißen	kleines	Pfund	Tasse

Exercise 4   Replace the pictures with the right words.

Ich hätte gerne ein Kilo a. ...., **ein Kilo**

b................................, **ein Pfund** c. ...., **ein halbes**

Pfund d. ...., **und drei Pfund** e. ....,

a.

b.

c.

d.

e.

Exercise 5 Change the phrases below into sentences. We've given you two examples

die grünen Äpfel ▸ Die Äpfel sind grün.
das schwarze Taxi ▸ Das Taxi ist schwarz.

a. die rote Kirsche ....

b. die kranken Kinder ....

c. der billige Ring ....

d. der durstige Mann ....

e. die schönen Souvenirs ....

f. die roten Äpfel ....

g. der weiche Pfirsich ....

h. die heiße Kartoffel ....

i. das kluge Mädchen ....

Exercise 6 *Opposites*

Fill in the right words from the box below. But watch out, there's one too many.

a. Ich bin nicht reich, ich bin ....

b. Diese Pfirsiche sind nicht weich, sie sind sehr ....

c. Der Tee ist nicht heiß, er ist ....

d. Dieser Ring ist nicht preiswert, er ist ....

e. Das Auto ist nicht neu, es ist ....

f. Diese Gläser sind nicht groß, sie sind ....

g. Der Apfel ist nicht süß, er ist ....

| teuer | hart | stark | klein | arm | sauer | kalt | alt |

Exercise 7   You want to buy a souvenir for a friend, a ring perhaps or something like that. You walk into a shop and talk to the sales clerk. We have printed her side of the dialogue below. Choose the right response from the scrambled phrases in the box.

a.   **Kann ich Ihnen helfen?**

....

b.   **Ja, wir haben Souvenirs.**

....

c.   **Wir haben Weingläser, Aschenbecher.**

....

d.   **Das kleine Weinglas, das kostet DM 12,50.**

....

e.   **Das große Weinglas, das kostet DM 16,80.**

....

f.   **Ja, wir verkaufen auch Schmuck. Wir haben Ringe aus Gold und aus Silber.**

....

g.   **Der Ring ist aus Silber mit Bergkristall und kostet 49 Mark.**

....

> **Und das große?**   **Der ist ja sehr schön.**
>
> **Und was für Souvenirs haben Sie?**
>
> **Aha. Verkaufen Sie auch Schmuck?**
>
> **Was kostet dieser Ring hier?**   **Haben Sie Souvenirs?**
>
> **Was kostet dieses kleine Weinglas?**

Exercise 8 You're in a souvenir shop looking at rings. Finish the dialogue below. The first answer has been filled in for you.

Useful word **bar** cash

a. **Wie finden Sie diesen Ring aus Gold?**
That one is too expensive for me.
   Der ist mir zu teuer.

b. **Und dieser Ring aus Silber?**
That one is very nice.

c. **Und wie paßt der Ring?**
That one is too big.

d. **Und dieser Ring hier?**
That one is too small.

e. **Oh weh. Und wie paßt dieser Ring?**
That one fits.

f. **Und der kostet nur 32 Mark.**
That's a very good price.

g. **Möchten Sie diesen Ring kaufen?**
Yes, I want to buy this ring.

h. **Wie möchten Sie bezahlen? Bar oder mit Scheck?**
By check, please.

Exercise 9 *Mismarriages!*

The paired-up words below got mixed up. Can you untangle them and put them together to form at least six new words?

**ANSICHTSBECHER   ASCHENKARTE   BRIEFGLAS
ELFENMARKE   GOLDBEIN   WEINSCHMUCK**

ANSWERS

Exercise 1

a. R **b.** F **c.** F **d.** R **e.** R

Exercise 2

You should have crossed out: **a.** oder Brot **b.** Pfund **c.** aus Silber
d. *either* großes *or* Kilo **e.** Flaschen **f.** Liter

Exercise 3

a. Pfund **b.** kleines **c.** halbes **d.** Glas **e.** Tasse **f.** weißen

Exercise 4

a. Karotten **b.** Zwiebeln **c.** Bananen **d.** Kirschen **e.** Trauben

Exercise 5

a. Die Kirsche ist rot. **b.** Die Kinder sind krank. **c.** Der Ring ist
billig. **d.** Der Mann ist durstig. **e.** Die Souvenirs sind schön.
f. Die Äpfel sind rot. **g.** Der Pfirsich ist weich. **h.** Die Kartoffel ist
heiß. **i.** Das Mädchen ist klug.

Exercise 6

a. arm **b.** hart **c.** kalt **d.** teuer **e.** alt **f.** klein **g.** sauer

Exercise 7

a. Haben Sie Souvenirs? **b.** Und was für Souvenirs haben Sie?
c. Was kostet dieses kleine Weinglas? **d.** Und das große? **e.** Aha.
Verkaufen Sie auch Schmuck? **f.** Was kostet dieser Ring hier?
g. Der ist ja sehr schön.

Exercise 8

b. Der ist sehr schön. **c.** Der ist zu groß. **d.** Der ist zu klein.
e. Der paßt. **f.** Das ist sehr preiswert. **g.** Ja, ich möchte diesen Ring
kaufen. **h.** Mit Scheck bitte.

Exercise 9

Here are some possibilities:
Ansichtskarte, Aschenbecher, Briefmarke, Elfenbein (ivory),
Goldschmuck, Weinkarte

Exercise 1 *Comparisons*

Compare the objects below, using the comparative form of the appropriate word in the box to describe the item picked out by the arrow; for example: **Dieses Auto ist schöner**.

weit	billig	groß	klein	teuer

a. **Dieser Rock ist** ....

b. **Diese** ....

c. **Diese** ....

d. **Dieses** ....

e. **Dieser Weg** ....

Exercise 2 *Riddles*

Find the words.

a. Österr O ch = ...

b. HS ҈ alen = ...

c. ☼ ̶t̶ag = ...

d. Däne (1 DM) = ...

Exercise 3

Paul wants to buy a pair of shoes, size 44, possibly brown or black, rather elegant, costing no more than DM 160,– . He's short of cash, so he wants to pay by credit card (**mit Kreditkarte**). Try to complete the dialogue below. Keep it as short as possible.

a. *Bitte schön*

b. *Welche Größe?*

c. *Und welche Farbe?*

d. *Möchten Sie etwas Elegantes oder etwas Sportliches?*

e. *Wie wär's mit diesem Modell? Es kostet 230,– .* !

f. *Und die hier, 149 Mark. Das ist ein Sonderangebot.*

cont.

g.

Exercise 4 *A vacation letter*

Study Anita's letter to Maria and check the correct answers in the multiple choice test below.

> Liebe Maria,
> viele Grüße von meinem Urlaub in der Schweiz. Es ist wunderschön hier, aber etwas kalt. Überall liegt tiefer Schnee. Leider bin ich im Moment krank. Ich liege seit zwei Tagen im Bett. Ich habe große Halsschmerzen und ein bißchen Fieber. Und seit heute morgen habe ich auch noch Ohrenschmerzen. Alles Gute und bleibe gesund!
> Deine Anita

a. Anita is on vacation
   □ in Austria
   □ in Switzerland

b. She
   □ doesn't like it very much
   □ thinks it's very beautiful there

c. There's
   □ lots of snow
   □ not enough snow

d. She's been sick in bed
   □ for four days now
   □ for two days now

e. She has
   □ a very high temperature
   □ a little bit of a fever

f. She is also suffering from
   □ an earache
   □ a headache

Exercise 5 The sign below tells you where to find certain items in a department store. Where would you go to buy the various articles below? Write either **Erdgeschoß** (ground floor), **1. Obergeschoß** (first floor) or **2. Obergeschoß** (second floor).

ERDGESCHOSS
Parfümerie
Uhren - Schmuck
Zeitschriften
Kurzwaren - Handarbeiten
Modewaren
Strümpfe - Handschuhe
Schreibwaren
Bücher
Süßwaren
Herrenartikel

1. OBERGESCHOSS
Lederwaren - Schirme
Jeans / Sportswear
Badebekleidung
Herren- und Knabenbekleidung
Damen- und Mädchenbekleidung
Strickwaren
Babyartikel
Miederwaren

2. OBERGESCHOSS
Gardinen
Heimtextilien
Bettwaren
Alles fürs Bad

a. Candy

....

b. A watch

....

c. Baby clothes and equipment

....

d. Sportswear

....

e. Bed linens

....

f. Swimwear

....

g. Bathroom articles

....

h. Home textiles

....

i. Jewelry

....

j. Ladies' wear

....

Exercise 6 *A riddle*

You might be able to guess the answer in English once you've goten the idea. You will get the German answer by doing the exercise below. To give you a clue: it's something that can be heard from just about every church tower.

Useful words   **Zunge** tongue
Freud(e) joy
teilnehmen to take part

Ich spreche ohne Zunge
Ich singe ohne Lunge
Ich hab kein Herz
und nehm doch teil an Freud und Schmerz.

a. 250 ⟦1⟧ ☐ ☐ ☐ Aufschnitt

b. zwei ⟦2⟧ ☐ ☐ ☐ Milch

c. drei ☐ ☐ ☐ ⟦3⟧ Zwiebeln

d. eine ☐ ☐ ⟦4⟧ ☐ ☐ ☐ Taschentücher

e. ein ☐ ☐ ☐ ⟦5⟧ Kuchen

f. vier ☐ ☐ ☐ ☐ ☐ ⟦6⟧ ☐ Wein

Keyword: ....

Exercise 7   Here is an ad from the local paper. Which of the items on your shopping list could you get on sale? Check them off the list.

Karwendel Naturkäsescheiben
Gouda, Edama, Tilsiter, **150g**; Emmentaler, **100 g**;
Aufschnitt, **125 g**;
48/40/45% Fett i. Tr.
jede Packung **1.99**

Blend-a-med oder Antibelag Zahncreme
jede 75 ml Tube **2.19**

Danke Küchentücher
4 x 65 Blatt **3.57**

Saupiquet Thunfischstücke in Öl
210 ml Dose **1.39**

Erlauer Spätburgunder
Rotwein
0,75 l Flasche **2.79**

Viss Haushaltsreiniger
500 ml Flasche **2.49**

Pott Rum   40% Vol.
0,75 l Flasche **12.99**

Softis Taschentücher
30 x 10 Stück
Packung **4.79**

Danke Toilettenpapier
3-lagig
8 x 200 Blatt **5.55**

Noris Wein-brand
36% vol.
0,7 l Fl. **9.99**

Wesergold Orangensaft oder Apfelsaft
1 l Packung **-.89**

cheese
toilet paper
toothpaste
tissues
brandy
rum
salami
apple juice
oranges
bread
red wine
white wine
tuna

ANSWERS

Exercise 1

a. Dieser Rock ist teurer. **b.** Diese Katze ist kleiner. **c.** Diese Schuhe sind billiger. **d.** Dieses Kind ist größer. **e.** Dieser Weg ist weiter.

Exercise 2

a. Österreich **b.** Sandalen **c.** Sonntag **d.** Dänemark

Exercise 3

a. Ich möchte ein Paar Schuhe. **b.** Größe 44 **c.** Braun oder schwarz **d.** Etwas Elegantes **e.** Das ist mir zu teuer! **f.** Die nehme ich. **g.** Kann ich mit Kreditkarte bezahlen?

Exercise 4

a. In Switzerland **b.** thinks it's very beautiful there **c.** lots of snow **d.** for two days now **e.** a little bit of a fever **f.** an earache

Exercise 5

a. Erdgeschoß **b.** Erdgeschoß **c.** 1. Obergeschoß **d.** 1. Obergeschoß **e.** 2. Obergeschoß **f.** 1. Obergeschoß **g.** 2. Obergeschoß **h.** 2. Obergeschoß **i.** Erdgeschoß **j.** 1. Obergeschoß

Exercise 6

a. Gramm **b.** Liter **c.** Kilo **d.** Packung **e.** Stück **f.** Flaschen
Keyword: **Glocke** (bell)

Exercise 7

You should have checked off all items except salami, oranges, bread, and white wine.

Exercise 1   *Find the difference*

Study the tickets and decide whether the statements below are **richtig oder falsch**.

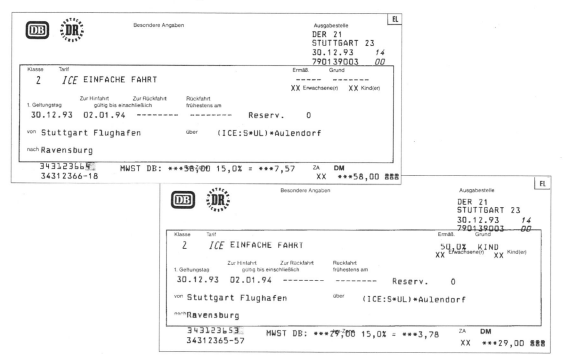

a.	Both are from Stuttgart airport to Ravensburg.	R F
b.	One is first class, the other is second class.	R F
c.	Both tickets are valid for return trips.	R F
d.	One ticket is for one adult and one for a child.	R F
e.	One ticket costs DM 58,–, the other DM 29,–.	R F
f.	Both tickets cost DM 30,12.	R F
g.	Both tickets include an ICE-surcharge.	R F

Exercise 2   A passenger is asking about the next train to Munich and the fares. Put the dialogue below in the correct order and write it out correctly. Use a separate piece of paper if necessary.

Passenger:
a.   Einfach.
b.   Ist das ein ICE-Zug?
c.   Wann fährt der nächste Zug nach München?
d.   Gut, dann möchte ich eine Fahrkarte nach München bitte. Mit ICE-Zuschlag.
e.   Und was kostet der ICE-Zuschlag?

Official:
A   Ja, das ist ein ICE-Zug.
B   Einmal München einfach mit ICE-Zuschlag, das macht 69,50 Mark.
C   Der ICE-Zuschlag kostet 10 Mark.
D   Einfach oder hin und zurück?
E   Der nächste Zug nach München fährt um 14.20 Uhr ab.

....

....

....

....

Exercise 3   *Journeys*

Complete the crossword puzzle – all the words have to do with travel; the keyword is the name of a city that has one of the biggest airports in Europe.

a.   Mode of transportation
b.   You're avoiding a fare if you haven't got one
c.   Where you catch the plane
d.   German for 'connection'
e.   The first is more expensive than the second
f.   This happens right at the end
g.   Sometimes it pays to have a little extra
h.   This ticket will guarantee you a seat
i.   ... and you'll be very sorry if you miss it.

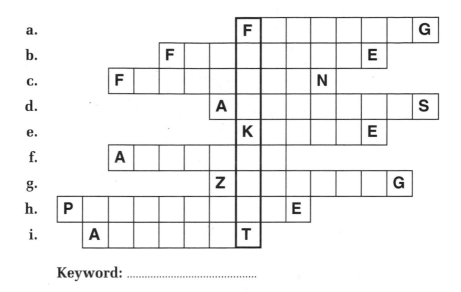

Keyword: ....

Exercise 4 *Informed guesses*

Match the signs with the translations. You won't need to know every word to figure things out.

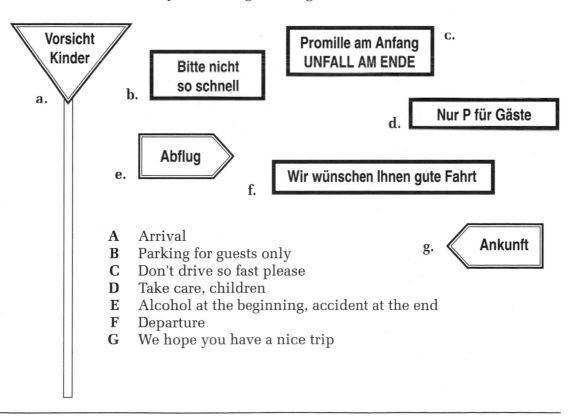

- **A** Arrival
- **B** Parking for guests only
- **C** Don't drive so fast please
- **D** Take care, children
- **E** Alcohol at the beginning, accident at the end
- **F** Departure
- **G** We hope you have a nice trip

Exercise 5 This is a typical printout you'll get when buying a train ticket. It gives details of the next connection to your destination, in this case from Stuttgart airport to Ravensburg via Ulm. Study it, then answer the questions in English.

```
        STUTTGART FLUGHAFEN     NACH  RAVENSBURG           DIREKT N        PKZ 1
UEBER                           UEBER                      SCHLAF-/LIEGEWAGEN N

BAHNHOF                   UHR   ZUG        BEMERKUNGEN
Stuttgart Flughafen    ab 19:31 S
 Stuttgart Hbf (tief)  an 19:58
 Stuttgart Hbf         ab 20:12 ICE   599  Zugrestaurant
 Ulm Hbf               an 21:05
                       ab 21:12 E     3119
Ravensburg             an 22:07
```

a. When does the train leave Stuttgart airport?

....

b. What kind of train is it?

....

c. What time does it arrive at Stuttgart's main station?

....

d. What time does the train leave Stuttgart station?

....

e. What type of train is it?

....

f. Does it have a restaurant?

....

g. What time does it arrive in Ulm?

....

h. Do you need to change trains in Ulm? If so, what train do you take?

....

i. When does the train arrive in Ravensburg?

....

Exercise 6   Max needs to fly to Paris. He asks Herr Maier about travel details. Fill in the right words from the box below.

Herr Maier   a. .... **ich Ihnen helfen?**

Max   **Ich** b. .... **gerne nach Paris fliegen.**

Herr Maier   **Und wann** c. .... **Sie gerne fliegen?**

Max   **Am liebsten am Wochenende.** d. .... **Sie mir sagen, ob ich am Freitag abend eine Maschine nach Paris bekomme?**

Herr Maier   **Ja, es gibt eine Maschine um 19.30 Uhr.**

Max   **Gut, die nehme ich.**

Herr Maier   **Aber Sie** e. .... **jetzt gleich buchen. Die Maschine wird immer schnell voll.**

Max   **Gut,** f. .... **ich mit Kreditkarte bezahlen?**

Herr Maier   **Ja, selbstverständlich** g. .... **Sie mit Kreditkarte bezahlen.**

können	möchte	kann	müssen
möchten	können	kann	

Exercise 7   Do you understand this stamp for the United Nations Children's Agency Unicef? Try to translate the handwritten text.

Useful words   **Menschen** people
Mond moon
warum why
tun to do
sterben to die

100
Deutsche Bundespost
Wenn die Menschen bis auf den Mond fliegen können warum können sie dann nichts dagegen tun daß so viele Kinder auf der Welt sterben müssen?
40 Jahre
UNICEF Deutschland
1993

....

....

....

ANSWERS

Exercise 1
a. R **b.** F **c.** F **d.** R **e.** R **f.** F **g.** R

Exercise 2
Here is the correct sequence: **c.** E **b.** A **e.** C **d.** D **a.** B

Exercise 3
a. Flugzeug **b.** Fahrkarte **c.** Flughafen **d.** Anschluss **e.** Klasse
f. Ankunft **g.** Zuschlag **h.** Platzkarte **i.** Abfahrt
Keyword: **Frankfurt**

Exercise 4
a. D **b.** C **c.** E **d.** B **e.** F **f.** G **g.** A
Promille (literally 'per thousand') is a term used to describe alcohol
levels in the bloodstream.

Exercise 5
a. 19.31 **b.** suburban line (the 'S' under the heading **ZUG** stands for
suburban line) **c.** 19.58 **d.** 20.12 **e.** ICE **f.** yes **g.** 21.05 **h.** yes,
you need to take the E 3119 ('E' stands for Eilzug, a much
slower train) **i.** 22.07

Exercise 6
a. kann **b.** möchte **c.** möchten **d.** können **e.** müssen **f.** kann
g. können

Exercise 7
Here is a literal translation: If the people can fly as far as the moon,
why can't they do anything against so many children dying in this
world?

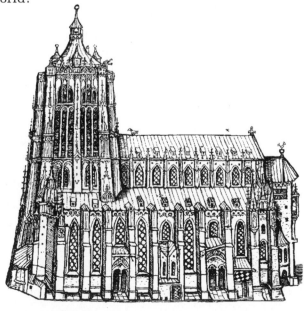

Exercise 1 Here's a page from a guidebook that gives you details of restaurants in Flensburg. Match the descriptions to the restaurants (you will need one restaurant twice).

Seit **Felsenkeller** 1889
1. Thüringer
Gasthausbrauerei
Weimar

Gebraut nach dem Reinheitsgebot aus dem Jahre 1516

RESTAURANTS

Flensburg hat eine Fülle von gemütlichen Kneipen, Cafés und Restaurants. Viele befinden sich in der Fußgängerzone und in den attraktiven Handelshöfen.

Alt-Flensburger Haus
Historische Gaststätte mit Antiquitäten (Schifferzimmer). Gemütliche Weinstube. Im Gewölbekeller werden historische Wikingeressen veranstaltet. Reichhaltige Speisekarte, auch vegetarisch. Sommergarten. *Norderstr. 8, Tel. 0461/2 64 64. Mo–Sa 12–14 Uhr und 18–23 Uhr, So geschl. Kategorie 2*

Brasserie Napoleon und Hofrestaurant
Zwei Antik-Restaurants im historischen Kaufmanns- und Theodor-Storm-Hof. Internationale Küche. Sommergarten. *Große Straße 42/44, Tel. 0461/1 31 10. Brasserie Mo–Sa 12–14.30 Uhr und 18–23 Uhr, So 18–23 Uhr. Hofrestaurant Di–Sa 18–23 Uhr, So und Mo geschl. Kategorie 2*

Chez Paul
Flensburgs Gourmet-Restaurant liegt direkt an der dänischen Grenze (4 km) im *Hotel an der Grenze*. Internationale Haute Cuisine in eleganter Atmosphäre. *Flensburg-Kupfermühle, Tel. 0461/70 20. Mo gschl., Di 18 bis 21.30 Uhr, Mi–So 12–14 Uhr und 18–21.30 Uhr. Kategorie 1*

Piet Henningsen
✪ Älteste Seemannsgaststätte Flensburgs am Hafen mit einmaliger Stimmung. Fisch. *Schiffbrücke 20, Tel. 0461/2 45 76. Mo–Fr 17–24 Uhr, Sa und So 11–24 Uhr. Kategorie 3*

Weinklause
✗ Kleine und gute Leckereien zu Wein und Bier im Dethleffsen-Hof. *Holm 45, Tel. 0461/2 11 55. Mo bis Fr 11.30–24 Uhr. Sa und So ab 11 Uhr Frühstück. Terrasse. Kategorie 3*

---

a. Small, good and delicious ....

b. Historical Viking banquets ....

c. Vegetarian food ....

d. Oldest sailor's bar in Flensburg ....

e. Elegant atmosphere ....

f. Two 'antique' restaurants ....

Exercise 2   *For small appetites only*

Study the snack menu, then choose the appropriate dishes for the requirements below and give a rough translation of the dishes you've chosen.

BROTZEITKARTE – Von 14.00 bis 21.00 Uhr

1 Paar Wienerle mit Brot	6,30	Gemischte Käseplatte mit Brot und Butter 13,30
Tomatenbrot mit Zwiebeln und Kräutern	7,30	Gemischte Schinkenplatte mit Brot
Bratenbrot garniert	8,00	und Butter 15,00
Käsebrot garniert	8,00	Allgäuer Vesperteller, Bergkäse,
Salamibrot garniert	8,50	Rauchfleisch, Brot und Butter 15,50
Wurstsalat mit Brot	8,50	
Schweizer Wurstsalat mit Brot	9,00	
Schinkenbrot roh oder gekocht	9,50	TOAST
Leberkäse mit Essiggurke und Brot	9,50	Hawaiitoast mit Schinken, Ananas und
Kalter Braten mit Essiggurke,		Käse 13,00
Brot und Butter	11,30	Bauerntoast mit Graubrot, Rauchfleisch,
Salatplatte mit Schinken und Ei	13,30	Tomaten und Käse 13,00

Useful words   **Wienerle**   type of hot dog
garniert   garnished
Leberkäse   special type of meat loaf
Essig   vinegar; here: pickled
Vesper   snack
Rauch   smoke(d)

a.   Which snacks are suitable for vegetarians?

....

....

....

b.   Which snacks would need to be avoided by someone who is allergic to cheese?

....

....

....

c.   Any dishes that don't come with bread?

....

Exercise 3 And now for the real thing. Soups, appetizers, and children's meals first. Study those three items on the menu below, then answer the questions by giving your menu suggestions in German with a short translation in English. (You will need a separate piece of paper for this exercise.)

SUPPEN

Kraftbrühe mit Maultaschen	4,20
Leberspätzlesuppe	5,00
Allgäuer Käsesuppe mit Brotcroutons und Kräutern	6,80

VORSPEISEN UND SALATE

Kleiner, gemischter Salat (nur als Beilage)	5,50
Gebackener Camembert mit Preiselbeeren und Toast	9,80
Gemischter, grüner Salat mit Schinken und Kräuterrahm	11,50
Krabbencocktail mit Toast und Butter	11,80
Räucherlachs mit Sahnemeerrettich, Toast und Butter	17,80
½ Forellenfilet mit Sahnemeerrettich, Toast und Butter	11,80

KINDERGERICHTE

Portion Spätzle mit Sauce	5,80
Portion Pommes frites mit Ketchup	5,50
Kinderschnitzel mit Rahmsauce und Spätzle	9,80
Kinderschnitzel, paniert mit Pommes frites	9,80

HAUPTGERICHTE

Zarter Wildschweinbraten mit Blaukraut und Semmelknödel	18,80
Poulardenbrust in pikanter Currysauce, Patna-Reis und grüner Salat	18,60
Schottischer Wildwasserlachs mit Basilikum und Crème fraîche, Broccoligemüse und Salzkartoffeln	25,80
Entenbrust, frisches Gemüse vom Markt und Gratinkartoffeln	27,80

DESSERT

Eisbecher mit frischen Kiwi und Sahne	7,80

Useful words **Kraftbrühe** meat broth
Lachs salmon
Ente duck
Brust breast
Poularde chicken
paniert breaded
Semmelknödel bread dumplings
zart tender
Meerrettich horseradish

a. Which soup would be suitable for vegetarians?

b. What would you order for a first course if you wanted a taste of seafood?

c. What would you order if you felt like having a piece of fish for an appetizer? (2 items)

d. Could you order just a salad for a main course?

e. Which main course for children has meat in it? (2 items)

Exercise 4 *The main course*

Take a look at the **Hauptgerichte** and **Dessert** on the menu and compare them to the statements below. Delete any items that do not appear in that particular dish.

a. The chicken comes with rice
   potatoes
   salad

b. The duck comes with vegetables
   salad
   potatoes

c. The wild boar comes with rice
   dumplings
   cabbage

d. The wild salmon comes with broccoli
   salad
   potatoes boiled in salt water

e. The dessert consists of fruit
   cake
   ice cream
   cream

Exercise 5 *Crossword*

What's the common letter in all the keywords?
Fill in the puzzle below.

a. **Wo kann man hier schnell** ....?

b. **Was ist die** .... **des Tages?**

c. **Was können Sie mir heute** ....?

d. **Ich hätte** .... **einen Wein bitte.**

e. **Gibt** .... **auch Ulmer Spezialitäten?**

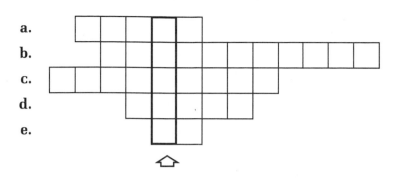

a.

b.

c.

d.

e.

⇧

Exercise 6 Find the one that doesn't belong.

a. **Rinderbraten**
   Schweineschnitzel
   Brathähnchen
   Fischfilet

b. **Forelle**
   Rostbraten
   Kalbsfilet
   Rumpsteak

c. **Kartoffeln**
   Reis
   Bratwurst
   Spätzle

d. **Pommes frites**
   Schweinshaxe
   Sauerkraut
   Junges Gemüse

e. **Bouillon mit Ei**
   Tomatensuppe
   Kraftbrühe
   Gemischter Salat

Weinstube

Haltnau

Meersburg
Inh. Werner Endres
Telefon 07532 - 97 32

Ruhetag Donnerstag

ANSWERS

Exercise 1
a. Weinklause   **b.** and **c.** Alt-Flensburger Haus   **d.** Piet Henningsen
e. Chez Paul   **f.** Brasserie Napoleon und Hofrestaurant

Exercise 2
a. Tomatenbrot mit Zwiebeln und Kräutern (bread topped with tomatoes, onions and herbs); Käsebrot garniert (bread with cheese and garnish); gemischte Käseplatte mit Brot und Butter (mixed cheese platter with bread and butter)   **b.** Käsebrot (as above); gemischte Käseplatte (as above); Allgäuer Vesperteller, Bergkäse, Rauchfleisch, Brot und Butter (Allgäu snack platter, mountain cheese, smoked meat, bread and butter); Hawaiitoast mit Schinken, Ananas und Käse (Hawaiian toast with ham, pineapple and cheese); Bauerntoast mit Graubrot, Rauchfleisch, Tomaten und Käse (farmer's toast with bread, smoked meat, tomato and cheese)   **c.** Salatplatte mit Schinken und Ei (salad plate with ham and egg)

Exercise 3
a. Allgäuer Käsesuppe mit Brotcroutons und Kräutern (Allgäu cheese soup with croutons and herbs)   **b.** Krabbencocktail mit Toast und Butter (shrimp cocktail with toast and butter)   **c.** Räucherlachs mit Sahnemeerrettich, Toast und Butter (smoked salmon with creamed horseradish, toast and butter) *or*: $1/2$ Forellenfilet (half a trout filet)   **d.** no   **e.** Kinderschnitzel mit Rahmsauce und Spätzle (children's schnitzel with cream sauce and Spätzle) *or*: Kinderschnitzel, paniert mit Pommes frites (children's breaded schnitzel with french fries)

Exercise 4
You should have deleted these items: **a.** potatoes   **b.** salad   **c.** rice **d.** salad   **e.** cake

Exercise 5
a. essen   **b.** Spezialität   **c.** empfehlen   **d.** gerne   **e.** es
Common letter: **e**

Exercise 6
a. Fischfilet (everything else is meat)   **b.** Forelle (everything else is meat)   **c.** Bratwurst (the only meat/sausage)   **d.** Schweinshaxe (the only meat)   **e.** Gemischter Salat (everything else is soup)

Exercise 1   Paul is interviewing Marion about her likes and dislikes. Study the dialogue, then decide whether the statements below are **richtig oder falsch**.

Paul   Was essen Sie gern?
Marion Ich esse gerne Nudeln, aber noch lieber mag ich Spätzle, und am liebsten esse ich Käsespätzle.
Paul   Wohin reisen Sie gern?
Marion Am liebsten reise ich nach Spanien, aber ich reise auch gerne nach Italien, und Portugal gefällt mir auch ganz gut.
Paul   Was trinken Sie gern?
Marion Am liebsten Badenwein, aber Frankenwein trinke ich auch gerne. Württemberger mag ich nicht so gerne. Die sind mir zu herb.
Paul   Gefällt es Ihnen in Hamburg?
Marion Ja und nein. Mir gefallen die vielen Geschäfte und Restaurants. Und die Leute sind auch ziemlich freundlich. Aber ich mag das Meer nicht. Ich komme aus dem Süden, und ich mag die Berge lieber.

a.	Marion doesn't like pasta.	R	F
b.	She likes Käsespätzle best of all.	R	F
c.	She likes traveling to Portugal best of all.	R	F
d.	She doesn't like traveling to Italy.	R	F
e.	She likes Württemberger but dislikes Frankenwein.	R	F
f.	Badenwein is her favorite wine.	R	F
g.	She likes Hamburg.	R	F
h.	She likes and dislikes Hamburg at the same time.	R	F
i.	There are too many shops and restaurants there for her taste.	R	F
j.	The people are friendly.	R	F
k.	She likes the ocean.	R	F
l.	She's from the south and prefers the mountains.	R	F

Exercise 2 *Find the ads*

Here are some clues – which establishment do they refer to?

a. This hotel is near the theater. ....

b. Greek specialities ....

c. If you want to sleep quietly, you have to go to the station.

....

d. A famous bar from the 16th century ....

e. Wines galore ....

f. Popular café at the Münsterplatz ....

g. ... right in the historic city hall ....

Exercise 3 Sabine is being interviewed about her life in Berlin. Study the short passage about her and answer the questions as she would answer them.

> **Sabine wohnt seit sechs Wochen in Berlin. Sie arbeitet jetzt bei der Hypobank. Ihre Arbeit gefällt ihr gut, und ihre Kollegen sind freundlich. Aber Berlin gefällt ihr nicht gut. Die Stadt ist zu groß für sie.**

a. **Seit wann wohnen Sie in Berlin?**
   Ich wohne seit...
....

b. **Wo arbeiten Sie?**

....

c. **Gefällt Ihnen Ihre Arbeit?**

....

d. **Und wie sind Ihre Kollegen?**

....

e. **Gefällt Ihnen Berlin?**

....

f. **Warum nicht?**

....

Exercise 4   Now Uwe asks Anna about her likes and preferences. He's on the other end of the phone, so we only transcribed Anna's answers. Try to reconstruct Uwe's questions from her answers and write them down. To make matters easier, we've written in one complete question and some other clues. Here are some expressions you'll definitely need: **was/wohin gern/am liebsten**.

Uwe   *Essen Sie gerne Spaghetti?*

Anna   **Ja, ich esse gerne Spaghetti.**

Uwe   *Was essen* a. ....?

Anna   **Am liebsten esse ich Pizza.**

Uwe   *Und was* b. ....?

Anna   **Ich trinke gerne Wein.**

Uwe   c. ....?

Anna   **Am liebsten trinke ich Champagner.**

Uwe   *Wohin* d. ....?

Anna   **Ich reise gerne nach Skandinavien.**

Uwe   e. ....?

Anna   **Am liebsten reise ich nach Schweden.**

gerne

lieber

am liebsten

Exercise 5 *Likes galore!*

All the statements below are about likes and preferences.
You'll need to use **gern/lieber/am liebsten** and **gut/besser/am
besten**. We've filled in some sentences to make it easier.
Use **gern** for **a.**, **b.** and **c.**, **gefallen** for **d.** and **e.**

*	one star means: you like it
**	two stars mean: you like it even better
***	three stars mean: you like it best of all

a. *Ich esse gern*   Kuchen.   *

.... *lieber* Sahnetorte.   * *

....Eis.   * * *

b. *Ich trinke* ....Wasser.   *

.... Saft.   * *

.... Cola.   * * *

c. *Ich reise gern*   nach Alaska.   *

.... nach Kanada.   * *

.... in die Antarktis   * * *

d. *Mir gefällt*   Paris   *gut* .   *

.... Rom ....   * *

.... Istanbul ....   * * *

e. *Mir* ....der Film ....   *

.... das Theaterstück ....   * *

.... das Buch ....   * * *

ANSWERS

Exercise 1
a. F **b.** R **c.** F **d.** F **e.** F **f.** R **g.** R and F **h.** R **i.** F **j.** R **k.** F
l. R

Exercise 2
a. Hotel Stern **b.** Ulmer Schachtel **c.** Bundesbahnhotel **d.** Zur
Forelle **e.** Dreikönigscafé **f.** Mohrenköpfle **g.** Ratskeller

Exercise 3
a. Ich wohne seit sechs Wochen in Berlin. **b.** Ich arbeite jetzt bei der
Hypobank. **c.** Ja, meine Arbeit gefällt mir gut. **d.** Meine Kollegen
sind freundlich. **e.** Berlin gefällt mir nicht gut. **f.** Die Stadt ist zu
groß für mich.

Exercise 4
a. Sie am liebsten? **b.** trinken Sie gern? **c.** Was trinken Sie am
liebsten? **d.** reisen Sie gern? **e.** Wohin reisen Sie am liebsten?

Exercise 5
a. Ich esse lieber Sahnetorte. Ich esse am liebsten Eis. **b.** Ich trinke
gern Wasser. Ich trinke lieber Saft. Ich trinke am liebsten Cola. **c.** Ich
reise lieber nach Kanada. Ich reise am liebsten in die Antarktis.
d. Mir gefällt Rom besser. Mir gefällt Istanbul am besten. **e.** Mir
gefällt der Film gut. Mir gefällt das Theaterstück besser. Mir gefällt
das Buch am besten.

Exercise 1 *The weather*

Match the correct captions with the appropriate pictures. But watch out, one of the six pictures can actually take two captions!

a.

d.

b.

e.

c.

f.

A	Es regnet	**E**	Die Sonne scheint
B	Es ist heiter	**F**	Starker Wind
C	Starker Nebel!	**G**	Es schneit
D	Es ist wolkig		

Exercise 2   *Weather mobile*

All the answers to the clues below have something to do with the weather.

a.   Too cold for tender plants
b.   It will cheer you up
c.   Necessary for skating
d.   Not a bad thing every once in a while
e.   Skiers like it
f.   Makes nice puddles
g.   You can't see through it, even if your vision is excellent
h.   Beyond them, the blue sky...

Exercise 3 *Find the words*

Here's a passage about the Baltic coast (**die Ostseeküste**). Not all the words will be familiar to you, but most of them are easy to guess from their context. See if you can write them down next to their English equivalents!

Die Ostseeküste

Die Ostseeküste ist eine solide, preiswerte Urlaubsregion. Weil vor allem Familien, Segler und Senioren dort ihre Ferien verbringen, nicht aber der Jetset, bleiben die Preise auch in der Hochsaison akzeptabel. Ein Privatzimmer ohne Frühstück kostet pro Nacht und Person zwischen zwanzig und dreißig Mark, eine Ferienwohnung mit zwei bis vier Betten achtzig bis hundert Mark. Auch Ferien auf dem Bauernhof sind günstig. Es gibt auch zahlreiche Campingplätze. Die Ostseeküste und ihr Binnenland hat für jeden etwas zu bieten. Die flache Landschaft ist ideal für Radtouren, das Meer, die Flüsse und die Seen sind ein Paradies für Angler. Segeln kann man nicht nur im Meer, sondern auch auf den vielen Binnenseen. Die vielen lokalen Feste sind eine gute Chance, um regionale Spezialitäten zu probieren.

a. vacation area ....

b. older people ....

c. high season ....

d. acceptable ....

e. flat landscape ....

f. bicycle tours ....

g. inland lakes ....

h. festivals ....

Exercise 4   Study the passage in Exercise 3, then decide whether the statements below are **richtig oder falsch**.

a.   The Baltic coast is good value for money. | R | F |

b.   Even the jetset goes there for a vacation. | R | F |

c.   But during the high season prices are quite unacceptable. | R | F |

d.   A private room with breakfast can be as little as DM 20–30 per person per night. | R | F |

e.   A vacation apartment with 2–4 beds costs DM 80–100. | R | F |

f.   The flat landscape is ideal for bicycle tours. | R | F |

g.   The sea, the lakes and the rivers are wonderful for fishing | R | F |

h.   However, sailing is restricted to the sea only. | R | F |

i.   There are many local festivals where you can sample the regional specialities. | R | F |

Exercise 6   Here's a letter from Anja, describing her home town Plön. Read it, then check the right boxes in the statements that follow.

Ich heiße Anja und ich komme aus Plön. Plön liegt in der Holsteinischen Schweiz, eine Region in Norddeutschland mit vielen idyllischen Wäldern und Seen. Plön ist ein ruhiges Städtchen mit zirka 10 000 Einwohnern. Es hat eine romantische Altstadt mit vielen kleinen Gassen und schönen alten Häusern. Das Plöner Schloß kann man nicht besichtigen, aber es gibt dort Ausstellungen und Konzerte. Im Schloßpark sind viele alte Linden, dort kann man schön spazierengehen. Vom Schloß-garten führt ein netter Weg zur Prinzen-insel, das ist eine Halbinsel, die sich 2 km in den Plöner See erstreckt. Nach der Wanderung kann man sich in einem Gasthof mit Hausmannskost stärken. Im Sommer kann man im See baden, das gefällt mir am besten. Auch mache ich immer wieder gerne eine Schiffsrundfahrt auf dem Plöner See.

a. Plön is
☐ a quiet, small town   ☐ a village

b. Plön lies in
☐ Switzerland   ☐ northern Germany

c. There are lots of
☐ high mountains   ☐ lakes   ☐ forests   (*check 2*)

d. There is a romantic old part of the town with
☐ little alleyways   ☐ an old museum
☐ beautiful old houses   (*check 2*)

e. You can still visit Plön castle.
☐ yes   ☐ no

f. There are concerts and exhibitions at the castle.
☐ yes   ☐ no

g. You can go for walks in the castle gardens.
☐ yes   ☐ no

h. The Prinzeninsel is
☐ an actual island and you can only reach it by boat
☐ a peninsula you can walk to quite easily

i. There is a good bar there, offering
☐ elegant cuisine   ☐ home cooking

j. What does Anja like best of all?
☐ swimming in the lake   ☐ sightseeing tours by boat

ANSWERS

Exercise **1**
a. B and E   **b.** A   **c.** G   **d.** D   **e.** C   **f.** F

Exercise **2**
a. Frost   **b.** Sonne   **c.** Eis   **d.** Schauer   **e.** Schnee   **f.** Regen   **g.** Nebel
h. Wolken

Exercise **3**
a. Urlaubsregion   **b.** Senioren   **c.** Hochsaison   **d.** akzeptabel
e. flache Landschaft   **f.** Radtouren   **g.** Binnenseen   **h.** Feste

Exercise **4**
a. R   **b.** F   **c.** F   **d.** R   **e.** R   **f.** R   **g.** R   **h.** F   **i.** R

Exercise **5**
a. a quiet, small town   **b.** northern Germany   **c.** lakes and forests
d. little alleyways and beautiful old houses   **e.** no   **f.** yes   **g.** yes
h. a peninsula   **i.** home cooking   **j.** swimming in the lake

Schloß Plön

Exercise 1 *Spontanurlaub* – *spontaneous vacation*

Fill in the correct past participles from the box below.

a. Ich habe mir gestern spontan eine Fahrkarte ....

b. Dann bin ich nach Wangen im Allgäu ....

c. Im Allgäu bin ich jeden Tag stundenlang .... ,
   jetzt bin ich topfit.

d. Ich habe in einem sehr schönen Hotel ....

e. Dieser Spontanurlaub hat mir wirklich sehr gut ....

> gefallen   gekauft   gewohnt   gereist   gewandert

Luftkurort
Wangen im Allgäu
Mittelalterliches Kleinod –
Wandern und Verweilen
in und um Wangen.
– Topogr. Wanderkarte
  M 1:25.000
– markierte Rad- u.
  Wanderwege
Fordern Sie
Informationen: Gästeamt im Rasthaus
          88239 Wangen im Allgäu, Telefon (07522) 74-211

Exercise 2   Write the appropriate passages from the text underneath the cartoons.

Ich stehe um halb sieben auf, frühstücke mit meinem Mann, lese die Zeitung und gehe um halb acht aus dem Haus. Ich fahre mit dem Bus zur Arbeit und bin dann von acht bis zwölf im Büro. Dann ist erst mal Mittagspause. Ich esse meistens in der Kantine, manchmal gehe ich auch in ein Café. Dann gehe ich im Park ein bißchen spazieren oder mache schnell ein paar Einkäufe. Mittags arbeite ich bis vier und fahre dann mit dem Bus wieder nach Hause. Mein Mann kommt gegen sechs Uhr nach Hause; um sechs gibt's das Abendbrot. Abends gehe ich gern ins Kino. Manchmal gehen wir auch ins Theater. Oder wir bleiben daheim und lesen oder hören Musik.

a. ....

....

b. ....

....

c. ....

....

d. ....

....

e. ....

....

f. ....

....

g. ....

....

h. ....

....

i. ....

....

j. ....

....

k. ....

....

l. ....

....

Exercise 3 *Urlaub*

Here are some extracts from the small ads in the German magazine *Freundin* describing various kinds of vacations, and four people in search of the ideal vacation. Which vacation would appeal to whom? Match them up.

Ich möchte mich gerne in Griechenland entspannen.

Samantha

Ich möchte gerne eine neue Sprache lernen.

Angela

Und ich möchte gerne in der Karibik segeln.

André

Ich möchte gerne in Italien malen lernen.

Toni

Angela: ....

Toni: ....

Samantha: ....

André: ....

Exercise 4 *Accommodation*

The syllables below can all be combined to form various terms you'll need to describe where and how you live. Write down as many as you can.

ORT	ZIM	WOH	
BAL	KÜ	MER	VOR
RUM	BAU	CHE	KON
ALT	NUNG	ZENT	

....

....

....

....

....

mit familiärer persönlicher Atmosphäre,

in der Fußgängerzone, mit Tagesbar, Halle, Fernsehraum, Sauna, Dampfbad, Solarium

Halbpension im Hotel Post

Fam. Alber   Tel. 28 48, Fax 28 48 50

Exercise 5 *A riddle*

Ich gehe alle Tage aus und bleibe doch in meinem Haus.

What is it? Clue: It's an animal. If you fill in the crossword by
unscrambling the anagrams below, the letters 1 to 8 will give
you the German answer to the riddle. All the words in the
crossword describe activities people do in their spare time.

a.   **ORTPS**
b.   **MMENSCHWI**
c.   **OBBYH**
d.   **GRAFOTOFIEREN**
e.   **ENFISCH**
f.   **SPRANECH**
g.   **SAMMELNBRIEFKENMAR**

a.

b.

c.

d.

e.

f.

g.

Keyword: ....

ANSWERS

Exercise 1
a. gekauft **b.** gereist **c.** gewandert **d.** gewohnt **e.** gefallen

Exercise 2
a. Ich stehe um halb sieben auf **b.** ...lese die Zeitung **c.** ...und gehe um halb acht aus dem Haus. **d.** Ich fahre mit dem Bus zur Arbeit **e.** Ich esse meistens in der Kantine **f.** ...manchmal gehe ich auch in ein Café. **g.** Dann gehe ich im Park ein bißchen spazieren **h.** ...oder mache schnell ein paar Einkäufe. **i.** um sechs gibt's das Abendbrot. **j.** Abends gehe ich gern ins Kino. **k.** Manchmal gehen wir auch ins Theater. **l.** Oder wir bleiben daheim und lesen oder hören Musik.

Exercise 3
Here are our vacation suggestions:
Angela: Sprachreisen or Mal- und Sprachferien Toskana und Elba (**Malferien** painting vacation)
Toni: Aquarellmalen or Mal- und Sprachferien Toskana und Elba
Samantha: Griechische Inseln – traumschön
André: Segeltörns auf gepflegten Yachten

Exercise 4
Here are some examples: Zentrum, Balkon, Wohnung, Altbau, Küche, Vorort, Zimmer

Exercise 5
a. Sport **b.** Schwimmen **c.** Hobbys **d.** Fotografieren **e.** Fischen **f.** Sprachen **g.** Briefmarkensammeln Keyword: **Schnecke** (snail)

TALKING ABOUT THE PAST

Exercise 1 *Crossword puzzle*

Kreuzworträtsel – diesmal auf deutsch. The boxed letters will give you the word for a place most young people love to visit.

a. Fluß durch Ulm
b. BMW ist eine deutsche...
c. Großes christliches Fest im Frühjahr
d. Ein sehr wichtiger Mann
e. Ein anderes Wort für Kneipe
f. Er geht zur Universität
g. Hier kann man Stücke sehen
h. Sehr wichtiger Faktor für den Urlaub
i. Hier kann man Filme sehen

a.
b.
c.
d.
e.
f.
g.
h.
i.

Schlüsselwort: ....

Exercise 2 Test your past tense by turning all the verbs in brackets into past participles and writing the full sentences in the spaces below.

a. Weihnachten bin ich mit einer Gruppe von Studenten in die Berge *(fahren)*

....

....

b. Am Tag haben wir Skifahren *(lernen)*

....

c. Abends sind wir immer ins Dorf *(gehen)*

....

d. Wir haben gut *(essen)* und gut *(trinken)*

....

e. Manchmal haben wir auch noch in der Disko *(tanzen)*

....

f. Und manchmal sind wir sehr spät ins Hotel zurück *(kommen)*

....

g. Wir haben auch einige Ausflüge *(machen)*

....

h. Und einmal haben wir eine berühmte Barockkirche in der Nähe *(besichtigen)*

....

....

i. Der Urlaub hat uns wirklich sehr gut *(gefallen)*

....

Exercise 3 *Visual clues*

Manche Menschen verbringen den Urlaub gerne auf einem

....

The first letters of each word will give you the keyword.

Exercise 4   *Vacations abroad*

Here's a short essay from Barbara about her last vacation.
Compare it with the English translation below and find the
differences. You should come up with seven mistakes
altogether – some are more subtle than others.

Im letzten Urlaub habe ich meine Freundin
in den U.S.A. besucht. Ich bin erst von
Frankfurt nach New York geflogen und
dort erst mal ein paar Tage geblieben.
Ich wollte in verschiedene Museen gehen
und auch ein Theaterstück am Broadway sehen. Dann fuhr ich mit dem
Bus nach Boston weiter. Dort wohnt meine
Freundin Ann. Wir haben viel gemeinsam
gemacht. Ihre Eltern haben ein Haus am
Meer, und ich habe sogar Wasserskifahren
gelernt. Das war rundum ein schöner
Urlaub. Nur leider war er viel zu kurz.

On my last vacation my girlfriend and I visited the USA. First
of all I flew from Frankfurt to New York and stayed there for a
few weeks. I wanted to do some shopping, and I also wanted
to see a play on Broadway. Then I flew to Boston where I met
up with my girlfriend, Ann. We did lots of things together. Her
parents have a house by the ocean, and I even learned how to
water-ski. All in all it was the best vacation of my life, but
unfortunately it was a little too short.

Exercise 5 *Back in town*

Put the right English captions underneath the pictures.

A And what is going on?
B The baker has closed
C I was away for only one year
D Even the butcher!
E I'd rather buy everything in the health food shop! Expensive but cozy!
F But that one there is too anonymous for me!
G It's supposed to have been slightly renovated!
H The grocery store

a. .... b. .... c. ....

....

d. .... e. .... f. ....

g. ....

from *Brigitte*, © Renate Alf

ANSWERS

Exercise **1**
a. Donau **b.** Firma **c.** Ostern **d.** König **e.** Lokal **f.** Student
g. Theater **h.** Wetter **i.** Kino Keyword: **Diskothek**

Exercise **2**
a. gefahren **b.** gelernt **c.** gegangen **d.** gegessen, getrunken
e. getanzt **f.** gekommen **g.** gemacht **h.** besichtigt* **i.** gefallen*
* Remember that verbs which already begin with **ge-** and verbs
beginning with **be-** do not add **ge-** in the past tense.

Exercise **3**
Visual clues: **B**ank, **A**uto, **U**hr, **E**is, **R**ose, **N**ase, **H**aus, **O**hr, **F**lasche
Answer: **Bauernhof**

Exercise **4**
Here is the complete correct translation:

On my last vacation I visited my girlfriend in the USA. First of all I
flew from Frankfurt to New York and stayed there for a few days. I
wanted to go to various museums, and I also wanted to see a play on
Broadway. Then I took the bus to Boston. That's where my girlfriend
Ann lives. We did lots of things together. Her parents have a house
by the ocean, and I even learnt how to water-ski. All in all, it was a
nice vacation. But unfortunately it was much too short.

Exercise **5**
a. C, A **b.** B **c.** H **d.** D **e.** F **f.** E **g.** G

Exercise 1   Study the travel tips from the *Marco Polo* guidebook on Lübeck and try to find the German phrases for the English expressions below – write them down.

MARCO-POLO-TIPS FÜR LÜBECK UND DIE LÜBECKER BUCHT

1 Lübeck
Die ganze Stadt ist ein Museum: Kirchen, Klöster, Stiftshöfe, Backstein und Marzipan (Seite 67)

2 Räucherkate in Harmsdorf
Die 300 Jahre alte reetgedeckte Räucherkate noch in Betrieb. Schinken satt! (Seite 76)

3 Ratzeburg
Schiffsfahrt von Lübeck nach Ratzeburg. Der Dom ist Norddeutschlands größter romanischer Backsteinbau (Seite 73)

4 Cismar
Künstlerdorf mit ehemaligem Benediktiner-Kloster. (Seite 76)

5 Güldenstein
Ein prächtiges von Wasser umgebenes Herrenhaus aus dem 16. Jahrhundert (Seite 76)

6 Gothmund
Ein verstecktes Fischerdorf an der Trave mit ländlicher Idylle (Seite 73)

7 Timmendorfer Strand
Im Nobelort der Lübecker Bucht gilt sehen und gesehen werden. Zwölf Monate im Jahr Betrieb (Seite 81)

8 Travemünde
Das Ostseebad mit Tradition hat nostalgisches Flair. Europas größter Fährschiffhafen (Seite 83)

a.   nostalgic flair   ....

b.   manor house from the 16th century

      ....

c.   with rural idyll   ....

d.   The whole town is a museum   ....

e.   fishing village   ....

f.   largest Romanesque brick building

      ....

g.   artists' village   ....

Exercise 2   The prefixes in the box below have come unstuck. Put them back in their right places.

a.   **Fred steht heute um sieben** ....

b.   **Ich gehe ins Kino. Gehst du** .... **?**

c.   **Wir haben nichts mehr zu essen im Haus. Bitte kaufe**

 etwas .... **!**

d.   **Hier ist Endstation. Ich steige jetzt** ....

e.   **Sven ist in der Küche. Er wäscht** ....

ab	auf	aus	ein	mit

Exercise 3   *wird* or *werden?*

Fill in the blanks.

a.   **Es** .... **kalt.**

b.   **Wir** .... **bald nach Hause gehen.**

c.   **Oh weh, Felix** .... **krank.**

d.   **Am Wochenende** .... **wir viel faulenzen.**

e.   .... **Sie mit dem Taxi zum Flughafen fahren?**

f.   **Nehmen Sie den Regenmantel, Herr Dompfaff, sonst**

 .... **Sie naß!**

g.   **Wir** .... **bis zum Sommer hier in dieser Stadt arbeiten.**

Exercise 4 *Rewriting the past*

This is what Renate did yesterday. Melina wants to copy her and do exactly the same today. Rewrite Renate's text in the present tense. As you know, you can use the present tense to indicate future plans in German. To make it easier, we have lined up all the phrases you'll need in the table below. But you might like to try to do the exercise without the extra help...

Gestern bin ich nach Berlin gefahren. Das Wetter war wunderbar. Zuerst habe ich die Gedächtniskirche besichtigt, dann bin ich zum Schloß Charlottenburg gefahren. Mittags habe ich in einem Restaurant gegessen. Am Nachmittag habe ich das Pergamonmuseum besucht, und abends bin ich dann wieder heimgefahren.

Heute fahre...

....

....

....

....

....

....

....

....

Und abends	~~fahre~~	~~ich~~	wunderbar
Mittags	fahre	ich	die Gedächtniskirche
Zuerst	fahre	ich	wieder heim
~~Heute~~	esse	ich	zum Schloß Charlottenburg
Das Wetter	besichtige	ich	das Pergamonmuseum
Am Nachmittag	besuche	ich	in einem Restaurant
dann	ist		nach Berlin

Exercise 5 Put the correct syllables together and write your newly formed words in the boxes below. Letters 1 to 10 will give you the word for something most people look forward to. To make it easier, we've filled in part of the puzzle for you.

WOH	SEUR	NUNG	SUCH	SEHEN	KON
PARK	BE	ZERT	FRI	TE	FREUN	FERN
STADT	DIN	LEU	AR	KNEI	BEIT	PE

a. | **W** | | | | | |
b. | **K** | 2 | | | | |
c. | **B** | | 3 | | | |
d. | **F** | | | 4 | | |
e. | **F** | | 5 | | | |
f. | **F** | | 6 | | | |
g. | **A** | | 7 | | | |
h. | **K** | 8 | | | | |
i. | **S** | | 9 | | | |
j. | **L** | 10 | | | |

Keyword: **W**..

Exercise 6 *Inviting Karin out*

Hans is trying to invite Karin out. Here is Karin's side of the conversation. Try to reconstruct Hans's questions. Write them down, using the familiar **du**. This is an open exercise: several different questions will be possible.

Hans .... ?

Karin **Nein, ich habe heute abend nicht frei.**

Hans .... ?

Karin **Nein, morgen abend habe ich auch nicht frei.**

Hans .... ?

Karin **Am Wochenende habe ich frei.**

Hans .... ?

Karin **Nein, ich habe noch keine Pläne.**

Hans .... ?

Karin **Ins Kino? Ja, gerne.**

Hans .... ?

Karin **Um acht, vor dem Café Gindele.**

Charlie Chaplin in Alaska
Goldrausch

USA 1925
Produktion, Buch und Regie: Charles Chaplin
Darsteller: Charles Chaplin, Mack Swain, Tom Murray, Georgia Hale u. a.
72 Min.   *besonders wertvoll*

LIVE

"Goldrush" läuft in der Originalfassung (engl. Zwischentitel), live begleitet am Klavier vom Stummfilmpianisten **Daniel Kothenschulte /** **Köln.**   DI.. 14.Juni

Exercise 7   *Die Qual der Wahl* – *Which one?*

Frau Wiese is not sure which of these 'lonely hearts' ads to respond to and writes to Frau Glück for advice. Who do you think would suit her best?

> Gentleman, Ende 30, kultiviert, Opernfan, liebt das Reisen und schönes Essen, sucht Partnerin.

> Romeo, kultivierter Mittvierziger, liebt klassische Literatur, Theater, Kino, Popmusik, schönes Essen, sucht seine Julia.

> Akademiker, Literaturprofessor, Mitte dreißig; Kino- und Opernfan, sucht reife Frau fürs Leben.

Liebe Frau Glück,

ich habe ein Problem. Ich suche einen Partner, und ich finde diese drei Anzeigen interessant, aber ich weiß nicht, wer der Richtige für mich ist. Ich bin geschieden, Anfang 40, und möchte gerne einen kultivierten Mann – aber er muß jünger sein als ich. Ich liebe junge Männer! Ich gehe gern in die Oper und ins Theater, und ich interessiere mich auch fürs Kino. Ich lese gerne klassische Literatur, und ich gehe gerne schön essen. Aber ich hasse Reisen. Welcher Mann ist wohl der Richtige für mich?
Danke für Ihre Hilfe!

Frau Wiese

ANSWERS

Exercise 1
a. nostalgisches Flair   **b.** Herrenhaus aus dem 16. Jahrhundert
c. mit ländlicher Idylle   **d.** Die ganze Stadt ist ein Museum
e. Fischerdorf   **f.** größter romanischer Backsteinbau   **g.** Künstlerdorf

Exercise 2
a. auf (**aufstehen** to get up)   **b.** mit (**mitgehen** to come along)
c. ein (**einkaufen** to buy/go shopping)   **d.** aus (**aussteigen** to get off)
e. ab (**abwaschen** to wash up)

Exercise 3
a. wird   **b.** werden   **c.** wird   **d.** werden   **e.** Werden   **f.** werden
g. werden

Exercise 4
Here are Melina's plans:

Heute fahre ich nach Berlin. Das Wetter ist wunderbar. Zuerst
besichtige ich die Gedächtniskirche, dann fahre ich zum Schloß
Charlottenburg. Mittags esse ich in einem Restaurant. Am
Nachmittag besuche ich das Pergamonmuseum, und abends fahre
ich wieder heim.

Exercise 5
a. Wohnung   **b.** Konzert   **c.** Besuch   **d.** Fernsehen   **e.** Friseur
f. Freundin   **g.** Arbeit   **h.** Kneipe   **i.** Stadtpark   **j.** Leute
Keyword: **Wochenende**

Exercise 6
Here are Hans's questions – yours might look a little different:

Hast du heute abend frei?
Hast du morgen abend frei?
Hast du am Wochenende frei?
Hast du schon Pläne?
Hast du Lust, ins Kino zu gehen?
Wann treffen wir uns?

Exercise 7
Here is Frau Glück's advice:

The gentleman wouldn't do because he loves traveling and she
hates it; the Romeo wouldn't do either because he's in his mid-forties
and therefore too old for her liking. So the literature professor would
be best: he's in his mid-thirties and looking for a mature woman...